**FREEPORT PUBLIC LIBRARY**
100 E. Douglas
Freeport, IL 61032

JUL 0 3 2014

P9-BZO-264

More praise for Carol Leifer and
*How to Succeed in Business without Really Crying*

"The only thing more impressive than Carol's success is how she has retained and polished all the lessons she's learned along the way. And the fact that she has decided to throw them your way for just a few bucks is such a ridiculously good opportunity for you, I can hardly believe it!"

**—JERRY SEINFELD**

"Carol is relentless, and an entrepreneur to the core. Read this book and learn! I have no doubt she will corner you if you don't!"

**—MARK CUBAN**

"I've been in the comedy business for 30 years and thought I'd seen and heard it all...until I read Carol's book! It's witty, classy, and filled with real-life advice gleaned from her years of getting laughs and enjoying success."

**—CAROLINE HIRSCH**
**FOUNDER OF THE LEGENDARY**
**NEW YORK COMEDY CLUB CAROLINES**

How to Succeed in Business Without Really Crying

BY

CAROL LEIFER

QUIRK BOOKS
PHILADELPHIA

Copyright © 2014 by Carol Leifer

All rights reserved. No part of this book may be reproduced in any form without written permission from the publisher.

ISBN: 978-1-59474-677-2

Library of Congress Cataloging in Publication Number: 2013911680

Printed in the United States of America

Typeset in Mrs Eaves and Gotham

Designed by Gregg Kulick
All photographs courtesy Carol Leifer
Production management by John J. McGurk


Quirk Books
215 Church Street
Philadelphia, PA 19106
quirkbooks.com

10 9 8 7 6 5 4 3 2 1

To my parents,
Anna and Seymour Leifer,
for imparting the gift of loving
what you do

# CONTENTS

# INTRODUCTION

When I was growing up, my only connection to show business was my Uncle Berni, who was a writer for the game show *Let's Make a Deal*. Berni and my Aunt Julie had a big house right by the ocean in Santa Monica (which seemed very exotic to a Long Islander). He was handsomely paid and always had great stories about "the biz." (He started out as an actor on Broadway!) My Grandma Becky even used to keep his "Written by" credit proudly framed on a table in her living room. To me, coming from a family of academics, this all seemed so mysterious and exciting. Which raised one question in my mind: How exactly do I get into this racket?

During my sophomore year of college, Berni told me he had a big-time television producer friend in Manhattan who was looking for a gopher and that I should call the guy when I was home for the summer. Maybe he would hire me over the break. So I called and set up an appointment to meet this producer in New York City.

But on the day of the meeting, extenuating circumstances reared their ugly head. First, I was forty-five minutes late because the Long Island Railroad was delayed. Second, I hadn't written down what floor this producer's office was on or his company's name (which was not the same as his name). So I had to ask a few people in the building before I could find his office. Third, I arrived sopping wet because it was raining and I didn't bring an umbrella.

When the producer called me in, we had what I thought was a nice enough meeting, during which I talked mostly about my college journey and my comedy aspirations. I left convinced I'd given a bang-up interview!

Well, I must say I was surprised a few days later when I heard that I hadn't gotten the job. "What gives?" I thought to myself. "I'm the niece of this guy's good friend, Berni Gould from California! Besides the fact that I'm a delight and a pleasure." But when I look back on it now, I cringe. How clueless was I, to think I'd be hired after showing up unforgivably late, vastly unprepared, and soaking wet to boot (not to mention dressed in a pair of jeans and a T-shirt)? On top of all that, I don't think I asked the producer even a single question—about himself or the job—during the entire interview. My reference point had been college, where on a daily basis it was all about me, me, me! And I never realized that looking for a job meant that I seriously had to reorient my entire perspective and behavior.

This book you're holding is the book I wish I'd had when I started out in my career. It's a collection of lessons I've learned since then, and although the industry I've persevered in happens to be the business of show, I believe those lessons are universal. Whether you've just embarked on the career you've always wanted or are already snarled in the struggle for success, I hope you'll find some useful counsel here.

But this book isn't only for people looking for career advice. If you're curious about the entertainment business, if you're a fan of comedy, or if you're the type of person who enjoys a good yarn about a plucky Long Island gal who went after her dreams, then this is the book for you. You'll find funny stories, some poignant moments, and hey, there's pictures.

And if my guidance can help just one reader avoid the career traps that I was unaware of—like, if it's cloudy on the day of your job interview, be safe and bring an umbrella—well then . . . let's hope that person has a huge Twitter following and can spread the word about where she got such great advice.

Performing in Wheatley High School's Varsity Revue, 1974.

PART
ONE

HOW TO HANDLE YOURSELF

DURING THE FRENZIED SCRAMBLE

FOR GAINFUL EMPLOYMENT

"Stand-up comedy is a
cash business, Carol. And
you can't beat cash!"
—Seymour Leifer, O.D.

# CHAPTER 1

## AND THE HAMMY GOES TO . . .

"Find a job you love, and you'll never work a day in your life." So goes the saying, and no truer words were ever spoken, except maybe "Never eat at an empty restaurant." I feel lucky that, even as a child, I knew I wanted to be in comedy. But there did come a day when I had to decide if I should stay on the comedy path or follow the road more traveled.

As a child growing up in East Williston on Long Island, New York, comedy was a natural interest for me. (As finding a husband would have been, except that it held no appeal to me for the same reason there's no Mrs. Anderson Cooper.) Comedy was revered in my house, as it is in many Jewish homes. Believe me, it's a long tradition of my tribe. Humor

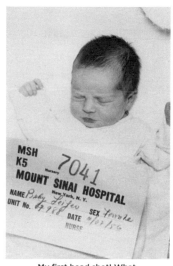

My first head shot! What, too much powder?

makes a great counterbalance to a history of persecution. And my late father, who was an optometrist (named Seymour—how perfect is *that*?), remains the funniest person I've ever known. I have yet to meet a pro who tells a joke better than he did.

Anna and Seymour Leifer,
the original comedy enthusiasts.

And he taught us well, my pop. Living in our household was the best comedy education anyone could have. My parents constantly played the popular comedy records (yes, kids, I did say records) of the time: *The 2000 Year Old Man* by Mel Brooks and Carl Reiner, Alan Sherman's *My Son, the Nut* (which included the hit "Hello Muddah, Hello Faddah"), *The First Family* by Vaughn Meader, various records by Mickey Katz (Joel Grey's father, who was a vaudeville performer), and the list goes on and on. But especially *The 2000 Year Old Man*, which we could recite line for line as it played. "Nectarines! Half a peach, half a plum, it's a helluva fruit!" My family and I were lip-syncing long before Britney Spears was born.

My dad would always call us all down from our rooms when the great comedians appeared on *The Ed Sullivan Show*. I watched the best—Jackie Mason, Rodney Dangerfield (whose HBO Young Comedians Special I would later appear on), a young George Carlin, Jackie Vernon—comedy kings of their time. And to this day, I can still remember the laughs that echoed in our family basement while we watched and listened to comedy. (Sure, on the Sullivan show we occasionally had to sit through Slavic people wearing tights and spinning plates on broom handles, but it was worth it.)

I would put on shows in our basement and go around the neighborhood door to door selling tickets (in the days when you could do that and not worry about getting your head chopped off). I went to sleep-away camp and enjoyed being considered the funny girl of summer. And I loved winning the camp's coveted Hammy Award, despite its non-Kosher status. In my heart, the Hammy rivals any of the big-time awards I've received as an adult.

As I got older, I became a serious fan of *I Love Lucy*, and I would watch reruns religiously every night. I came to know every episode and was a walking encyclopedia of the show. It was my first glimpse of sitcoms, and it left an indelible impression on me. (Note: In the comedy rooms I've worked in over the years, there seems to be a big dividing line re: *I Love Lucy*. I tend to find that women and gay writers worship the show, while straight male writers don't usually dig it.)

Even when I became a cheerleader in high school, my proudest moment was when the sketch we wrote and performed was the hit of the annual Varsity Revue. It was nice that we didn't have to spell out some jock's name while wearing Spandex to get noticed.

So it made sense that when I went to college in upstate New York (Seymour told me, "You can go to any school you like, Carol, as long as it's a state school!"), I would meet the guy who would forever change what I intended to do for a living. I was a theater major at Binghamton University (then named Harpur College)—which was about as practical as being a philosophy major—when I met Paul Reiser. He was in my dorm's theater group, Hinman Little Theater, and the funniest guy I had ever met (aside from my dad, of course). And Paul had a similar background to mine; he was raised in New York City in the same type of comedy environment. I discovered I wasn't the only nineteen-year-old who could recite *The 2000 Year Old Man* by heart.

We started dating, and Paul related his dream of becoming a stand-up comedian. During the summers, he would go to open-mic nights at comedy clubs, which were just becoming popular in New York City: places like the Comic Strip, Catch a Rising Star, and the granddaddy of them all, the Improvisation (a.k.a. the

Improv). Keep in mind, this was the late seventies; the stand-up boom with everyone and their mother doing five minutes in front of a brick wall was still years away. When Paul first told me he was performing at nightclubs, I must admit I thought, "Who is this guy, Vic Damone?" (Okay, younger readers, I'll just wait here while you google Vic Damone.)

At Harpur College, we'd sometimes spontaneously burst into song.

Paul Reiser in my dorm room. Ah, the days of the "Jewfro."

Jerry Seinfeld writing material in his first apartment.

Jerry emceed my first
audition at the Comic Strip.

So one night I watched Paul at his open-mic audition at Catch a Rising Star, and I was dazzled. Paul was really good at it—he was a natural. I decided to give it a try.

The scheduling was a simple process that remains in place to this day. You line up outside the club in the afternoon to get your "number," and later that night you go on according to the number you drew. It's what I've always loved about becoming a stand-up comic (that and not starting work until 8 p.m.). It was, and remains, uncomplicated. Get a number, go onstage, and voilà! You're doing stand-up comedy, my friend! (The self-loathing, regrets, jealousy—there will be plenty of time for all that later.)

So I put together five minutes of my best assumption of a stand-up comedy set. Stuff like, "Trident Gum. Their slogan is 'Four out of five dentists recommend sugarless gum for their patients who chew gum.' So who is this *fifth guy*? What's he recommending—rock candy and Jujubees?"

Not half bad. (I still have the tape of my first five minutes, and when I hear it, I feel like I'm listening to my *daughter*.)

As fate would have it, the emcee when Paul and I auditioned at the Comic Strip was an up-and-comer named Jerry Seinfeld. The emcee at Catch a Rising Star when I auditioned there was another comic who'd been at it for a couple of years named Larry David. They both gave Paul and me the thumbs-up, told us that we had passed the auditions . . . And that's how long I've known these guys—literally since my first day in show business.

So now we arrive at what was, or at least should have been, my first adult career dilemma. I had passed the audition at both clubs, but I still had a year left of college in Binghamton. (Paul was a year ahead of me and had already graduated.) So do I go back to school and defer my dream for a year? Graduating with a degree in theater seemed such an amorphous accomplishment. But the comedy clubs were giving me this real chance at starting in something new and exciting.

In fact, I never even debated the question. I decided to transfer to Queens College in New York City (a very tough school, by the way—you needed a pen to get in), finish my degree by day, and learn how to become a stand-up comedian by night.

To my surprise, my parents were immediately supportive. When I told my father that I'd passed the audition at the Comic Strip and wasn't sure about returning to college upstate, he swore, "Carol, you gotta strike while the iron's hot!" Even writing this now, I'm floored by his advice. At the time, I was a college junior who wanted nothing more than to seize the opportunity. But now, as a parent, I can hardly believe how cool, calm, and convinced my father was at that moment. Maybe his certainty came from never getting to live his own comedy dream, and he saw the possibility in me. Who knows? But I will always treasure how he and my mother were unwavering in their support for me to chase my dream.

At that point, I didn't think about what it would be like as a woman to enter the male-dominated field of comedy. It just never entered my mind. I attribute it to my upbringing. As far back as I can remember, my mother in particular instilled in me a fierce confidence—an assurance that I could do or be anything I put my mind to. What sex I was never entered the equation. Even to this day, when I'm challenged, I hear my mother's voice telling me to always believe in myself and trust my instincts.

My first time ever doing stand-up, as a college sophomore, in 1976.

My path after that decision, of course, wasn't easy. It rarely is for a stand-up comic. You bomb. A lot. I've had sets in rooms so quiet, a yoga class broke out. And you get heckled, which is unique to comedy. I've been to some operas, and no one ever yells, "Hey, fat boy! Yeah, you, the basso! You blow!" (But maybe it's because I've never been to an opera in Jersey.)

None of that mattered, though, because at the core of it all, I was just so happy doing what I love. I still perform at clubs around L.A. when I'm polishing up for a gig or trying out new material. And I don't earn a dime for it—occasionally, they'll give you something to eat if you've killed and they've got a kitchen. But there's nothing better than standing onstage with a mike in your hand telling jokes. My love for it hasn't changed from the first day I stepped in front of an audience. (Fortunately, my sense of fashion has . . . I hope.)

And by the way, here's a shout-out to being young—that's not a small part of my story. There's no way to explain it other than this: you lose your balls as you get older. Reality sets in, and man, is *that* a dream killer. So, for you readers at the beginning of your careers, take advantage of being young and brash and stupid. I look back and I can barely believe that I made such a bold decision—to transfer schools and become a stand-up comedian— without much thought. But that's the thing about passions; they tend to rule you. They're not hanging out at the punch bowl with Rational Thinking. (One caveat: Despite the heckling and bombing, I always got a lot of positive feedback about being funny, as did most of my comedic pals. So I would caution you about pursuing a dream if you find that, along the way, you're the only one clapping. Anything is worth a shot, but comes a time when you need to realistically evaluate your abilities.)

So, heed this advice: Find your true passion, even if it takes a little digging. Find the thing that's inside you, burning to get out. I've always loved the question "What would you attempt to do if you knew you could not fail?" (Hopefully it's not "fly a stunt plane without lessons.") Because the possibility of failure is the extinguisher that's always ready to douse your fire. Find work doing what you love, and whatever noisy doubts and distractions come along, your passion's voice will always rise above the din.

Go for it. Passion is an early riser. It will be out of bed and ready to work while indifference is still trying to get its pants on.

Meeting one of my comedy heroes, Mel Brooks! The late John Ritter
brought him over to our table at Orso in New York City.

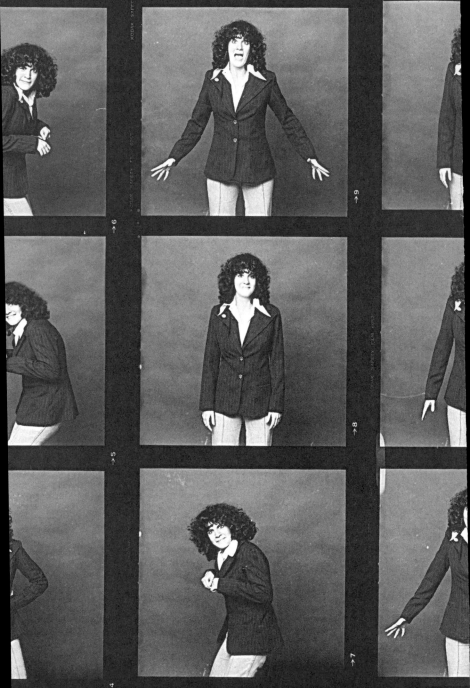

# CHAPTER 2

## MY BOSS WAS A DICK—EVEN
## WHEN YOU GOT TO KNOW HIM

So I'm living the dream . . . I'm a stand-up comic working in the greatest city in the world—New York! Only problem: money. I was making a cool five bucks a night. Cab fare.

A day job was a necessity so I could make my rent for a two-bedroom, fourth-floor walkup on Lexington Avenue, splitting the $450-a-month rent with my roommate Jim, a buddy from college who is still my friend to this day. At first I tried waitressing at the Comic Strip, which seemed logical—I was working there already anyway. But that turned out to be a disaster. Serving customers while trying to entertain them onstage was risky business, as I soon found out. The deadbeats figure out quickly that when their waitress is doing her set, it's a good time to skip out on the check.

One night as I was sharing my nightmare waitressing stories with a table of customers (also maybe not the brightest idea), one of them told me about a job opening she had heard about. A private eye was looking for a secretary. My eyes lit up! (Either out of excitement or because another of my tables looked like they were getting ready to bolt, I can't remember which.) She gave me a number to call, and I scheduled an interview for the next day at Foresight Security on Seventh Avenue.

I swear, I couldn't sleep that night, visions of 1930s black-and-white detective movies dancing in my head. Would the "dick" be wearing a fedora and call me "doll"? Would I soon be the gal "packin' heat" during the day while telling gags at night? (Would I be tomorrow's *New York Post* headline, after blindly heading to a job interview based on a tip from a woman who ordered a seven and seven?)

My bubble burst the second I walked into the waiting room, which was filled to the brim with a collection of slouchy, slack-jawed gum-snappers. I thought, "Is this defeated assortment really my competition for the gig? What gives?"

Turns out they were clients. The bulk of this company's business was administering polygraph tests to job applicants, from Burger King cashiers to hookers at escort services (I guess at both places, you want to make sure you get the order right). The opening was for a typist, operating a Dictaphone (a now old-fashioned device that was clearly named by a frustrated comedy writer). Basically the job was transcribing polygraph results onto paper. Miss Marple I would not be.

I might have turned around and gone home, disappointed. But I sensed an opportunity.

First, I was already a helluva typist (thank you, Mr. Feldman, my high school typing teacher!). Then during the interview with George, the boss/private eye (who was fedora-less, I might add), I raised the subject of possibly being creative with my hours. As a struggling comic, I was not yet getting the plum time slots at the club (1:10 a.m., 1:30 a.m, etc.). So I asked George how he would feel about my working eleven to six, with no lunch break, instead of nine to five? That way, I could get enough sleep when I got home from the club at night.

George went for it. I'm still not exactly sure why, but I'm grateful to this day. If he had said no, I probably would have taken the job anyway. But I must admit that my mother's advice was ringing in my ear as I sat down for the interview: "You don't ask, you don't get, Carol!" (An entire chapter in *The Big Book of Jewish Advice*, I expect.)

I worked at Foresight ("Where Your Security Is Our Concern!") for almost two years until I was finally making (barely) enough to support myself with stand-up gigs alone. A hundred bucks from Baruch College for a nooner! (Which is not what it sounds like—it's a daytime show at the student union.) The typing job was a lifesaver, thanks to the hours George let me work. But I must admit, I kind of enjoyed it. Nothing like a day's worth of mindless typing to clear the head for an evening of nightclub hijinks. (Although I wish just once someone would have called me a "dame with nice gams.")

Which is all a way of teeing up my advice for this chapter: Get creative with your job search. Whatever conventional means you use when seeking work, there are always ways to go off the grid, and I highly recommend that route. Where everybody zigs, zag. (And vice versa, in deference to zagging.) Here are four general principles to follow.

## 1. Get into the "machine."

Not surprisingly, a lot of people ask me how to get into writing for television. The stock answer is pretty basic: Learn how to write a "spec" script and then try to get an agent who could submit it for a job. But to me that's lousy advice, because I think your odds of getting a job in that way as a novice are practically zero. It's just too big a mountain to climb with baby steps like that.

So my recommendation, when people ask that question, is to try to get a job, any job, on a television show you love. There's not a show out there that doesn't have an extensive support staff of production assistants (P.A.s) and runners. It's low-paying work, you work crazy hours, and odds are good that at least one of the people in front of the camera will be a total psychopath. But that's not what matters in this equation. *You're there*, and that is priceless.

I believe this same strategy will work in almost any business— just get yourself on the premises, as close to the action as possible, in one of those grunt-level assistant gopher-type positions. You want to be someone who, like a production assistant, gets an insider's view of how the industry works. P.A.s do everything from getting more paper at Staples, to going on Starbucks runs (sometimes two or three times a day), to waking an actor in his dressing room, to taking the executive producer's dog to the groomer. Anything and everything, all the little stuff that the people stuck in that damn room writing all day have no time to do. I've sent P.A.s to the grocery store with the mandate, "Get at least ten different types of candy bars and bring them back." We writers love our sugar and caffeine.

So look for that entry-level job that allows you to be around the nucleus of the most influential employees. Especially one in which you'll have opportunities to do, and do well, what the career staffers shudder to do. Interacting with the staff is what it's all about, so being stuck in a mailroom or warehouse all day probably won't help you. A good head start is to apply for a college internship at your favorite show or business or wherever you're looking to work. I've seen so many people over the years climb the ranks starting as a lowly intern. For would-be television writers, I suggest you pick up a phone and call the main line of your dream show, or the network the show is on, and ask for information about its internship program. I suspect the direct approach will yield good results in other industries, too. The Internet is busting with all this info, or at least clear paths to finding it. (Check out IMDB.com.)

Job seekers, this is a good spot to raise the issue of working on your people skills, which are critical from day one. In television, a production assistant who's entertaining and likable will be kept around just because her personality is fun. Doesn't that work in every place of business? Larry David and Jerry Seinfeld, in hiring new writers for *Seinfeld*, always referenced "the easy hang." Whatever business you're in, you've got to be good at what you do. But you also need to be the easy hang, a person whom people like to be around and hang out with. It doesn't matter how talented you are if your personality is a drag. Or as one agent told me when I was just starting out: "Don't be an asshole. If you are, they'll fire you and hire someone who isn't."

However you wrangle it, I can't emphasize enough how great it is to get a foot on the same ground as your dream job. So many writers I know started out as a writer's assistant. They were good typists (Mr. Feldman, once more, big props) and then went on to learn the mechanics of computer script writing. It's a really clever choice, because as a writer's assistant, you're in "the room" with the writers all the time, taking down everything they're saying. They're not always the best-groomed group, but hey, you pick up so much about a job purely through osmosis. Being in the room is the best training ground a would-be TV writer could possibly have. So whatever career you're trying to crack into, figure out which room you need to be in, then pursue the job that will put you there.

## 2. Invest in opportunities that pay off later.

A paycheck is important, of course. But when the right opportunity comes along, don't be afraid to work for free if there's the potential for a bigger payoff in the future. An internship is one example, but be alert for other chances to show what you can do.

Little story: I was writing a pilot whose lead character was a female attorney, and I needed some help with the legalese. One of my cousins who's an attorney recommended a colleague, Sue (not her real name but seems like a good choice for a lawyer), who specialized in the type of law my character practiced. When my draft was finished, I sent it to her to catch any legal mistakes. Sue sent it back, with some joke pitches throughout the script. Some of her lines were phenomenal. I used a bunch in the final draft, they were that good. One of them I even anointed the "blow" (the last line in a scene, the one that's got to wrap up everything with a bang). Sue appreciated the praise, and when I thanked her, she told me she had always wanted to get into comedy.

So a few months later I sent Sue an e-mail asking if she wanted to read another script and maybe add some jokes again. Sue wrote back that she would be happy to, but she wanted me to pay her. I tried to explain how writers usually work in a pilot situation: you ask for input, and then when/if the show gets on the air, you can potentially hire that person as compensation. Sue didn't budge, which was certainly her prerogative. But I do think it was a lost opportunity for her. If Sue threw me some great jokes again, I would have seriously considered hiring her if the show had been picked up. So the moral is, don't always evaluate an opportunity as an immediate paycheck. Sometimes much bigger things might lie ahead if you sit tight and are patient.

## 3. Be a "squeaky wheel."

No other credo could better describe how an annoying crank caller wound up as one of only three writers for *The Howard Stern Show*.

If you're a Stern fan like me, you already know the story. And if you don't, it's pretty remarkable. Sal Governale was a stock broker who regularly called in to the show. He broke the chops of the producer, Gary Dell'Abate, by repeatedly pranking him, winding up the call with the pronouncement that Gary was a "horse-tooth jackass."

But what Sal really wanted was to write for the show. And as my fellow Long Islander told me, he just kept creating bits and submitting stuff: roast jokes, song parodies, material of all kinds.

Here's what I love most about this story: Sal just wore them down. He knew he had what it took to create comedy for the show, and he kept cranking it out. Eventually, they offered to try him out for a month. That month became ten years, and he's still at it.

As Sal told me himself, he was "relentless," and that's what it takes. His balls made him a permanent fixture on the show (and continue to, for he has no shame in endlessly offering them up in the name of entertainment value). Rock on, Mr. Governale.

Of course, aside from the Stern show, calling someone a jackass on a near-daily basis isn't a viable option for most job hunts. So you'll have to figure out what "relentless" means for your particular career path. Perhaps it's sending project pitches and samples of your work to managers and H.R. departments, so you'll already be on their radar when a job opens up. Maybe it means going to job fairs and networking sessions and other events so that you become a familiar face. A big part of the Governale strategy, though, is not taking no for an answer . . . the first time, or the first fifty times.

## 4. Use every "in" available.

When it comes to landing a job, there's no such thing as "unfair advantage." If you have some kind of connection that might grease the wheels, by all means *use it*. Though I will add this caveat: using that "in" comes with great responsibility. Because when you use someone else as your entrée, their reputation becomes part of the mix. Your connection is giving his or her word that, going forward, you will step up one hundred percent for whatever is asked of you.

So if you show up late to your interview, or do any of the other dumb stuff I warn you not to do (see Chapter 4, "So I Stole Soda from Aaron Spelling"), your benefactor's ass is on the line, too. If you mess up, the person who helped you will be screwed; he or she could lose all credibility with that contact. Which is exactly why I don't pull a lot of those kinds of favors anymore, unless it's someone I know and can vouch for personally. I've been burned way too many times doing a solid for a "friend of a friend."

Bottom line: No matter what your dream job is, don't hesitate to try something new or different to get it. Don't feel you have to follow the normal route. Try going off road. While everyone else is fumbling with their GPS, you just might reach the destination first.

With Paul Reiser outside my first apartment in New York City, 1978.

# CAROL LEIFER

## Actress/Comedian

Height:  5'5"          Hair:  Dark Brown          Eyes:  Blue

**CURRENTLY APPEARING:**

    The Improvisation - Hollywood, Ca.
    The Comedy Store - Hollywood, Ca.

**TELEVISION:**

    " Late Night with David Letterman"
    " An Evening at the Improv"
    " The Big N.Y. Laff Off" - Showtime
    " The Toast of Manhattan" - ABC pilot
    " Good Morning New York" - WABC N.Y.
    " No Soap, Radio"
    " Book of Lists"

**REGIONAL & STOCK:**

    " Fiddler on the Roof" . . .Tzeitel
    " You're a Good Man, Charlie Brown".. .Lucy
    " Story Theatre"....Henny Penny
    " You Can't Take It With You" . . .Mrs. Sycamore
    " Bye, Bye Birdie". . .Kim

**COLLEGE AND CLUB PERFORMANCES:**

| | |
|---|---|
| Catch A Rising Star | Dartmouth College |
| The Comic Strip | Colgate University |
| Comedy & Magic Club | Rutgers University |
| Diplomat Hotel | Vassar University |
| Dangerfield's | Fordham University |

**TRAINING:**

| | | |
|---|---|---|
| Acting | B.A. Theatre | Queens College, N.Y. |
| | Ron Orbach | Warren Robertson Theatre Workshop |
| Improvisation | Century Theatre Players, N.Y. | |
| Voice | Stephanie Tisheff Studio, N.Y. | |

Resume, 1982.

# CHAPTER 3

## DESPERATELY SEEKING SOUPY

Waiting to audition for a TV show is one of the most anxiety-producing feelings ever. Especially for me, because I sucked at it big time. You sit in a "cattle call" room with dozens of people, all thinking the same thing: "I hope these other numb-nuts fall flat on their face." It's positively life-affirming.

It's way worse for comics, because we are not built for auditioning. It's exactly why we picked our chosen field. Stand-up comedy may be the quintessential tightrope act (outside, of course, actual tightrope walking), but comics have all the control, which is ultimately what's most important to us. And stand-ups almost always have issues about "proving ourselves." We're only as good as our last set or joke. None of those things make it easy to put yourself at the mercy of a casting director. But only a month after I moved out to L.A., an audition came my way, and I was dying to get the part.

Director Barry Levinson, hot off the success of his film *Diner*, was casting a pilot for ABC. The show was called *The Toast of Manhattan*, and it was a comedy set backstage and behind the scenes of a variety show, à la *The Carol Burnett Show* (for which Barry had written back in the day). They were looking for comedians and actors who could do improv. It was a show that everybody in comedy wanted on their resume.

My agent told me the audition was simple: Go in and do a bunch of characters. That immediately put me at ease because I wouldn't be reading lines from a script. And when I went into the audition, a very relaxed vibe already permeated the room. Which normally didn't happen, at least not for me. (That's another thing traditionally hard for comics: being in the moment and going wherever it leads you—i.e., not being in control.) Then one of the producers, Rudy De Luca (whom I recognized from a couple of Mel Brooks movies) began improvising with me as one of my characters. We moved on to my other characters, and the interaction stayed pretty seamless; we just kept riffing together. (The steady round of laughs I was getting didn't hurt either. Those are the waves in a comedy audition that keep you buoyant.)

When the audition ended, we naturally moved into shooting the crap. Being a huge Mel Brooks fan, I told Barry that I loved his cameo in the movie *High Anxiety*. (He and Mel have an unforgettable scene, where Mel as Dr. Thorndyke uses a rolled-up newspaper to murder Barry, playing the pesky bellman.) I could tell that when I mentioned this cameo, I really struck a chord. Barry lit up and clearly felt complimented that out of all the things he'd achieved and accomplished, I remembered this small but hysterical part he had played. (By the way, it's so nice to tell someone in Hollywood that you love his or her work and really mean it.)

Lo and behold, I got the part. Alongside my good friend Paul Reiser, I was lucky enough to be a member of an eclectic cast that included Gilbert Gottfried and Craig T. Nelson. Who knows what put me over the top in that extremely competitive situation? I was up against so many talented people. But I don't doubt for a second that my quirky, out-of-left-field compliment to Barry Levinson sealed the deal. I love this story, because my obsession with comedy—which goes with me everywhere—may have been just the thing that landed me this unbelievable gig.

As a side note, we shot *The Toast of Manhattan* in May 1982, and it remains one of the most fun experiences I've ever had. The program didn't get picked up, but I made four thousand dollars, which sustained me for quite a while as a new transplant to Los Angeles. And being cast in a pilot—even though it didn't go forward—made my agent's job that much easier because a network had already deigned me "castable."

The lesson is there's no substitute for natural love and enthusiasm. Whatever it is that draws your passion, when you can turn it into your profession, you've solved one of life's greatest riddles. ("Love what you do" pops up a lot in these pages for a reason. Although it's not the advice I'd give to the stars of *Teen Mom*.)

What we're really talking about here is fandom. And the beauty of being a fan is that the enthusiasm is infectious. For example, I have a passing fancy for Broadway. I don't know much about it, but I grew up with my parents listening to cast albums, so that world always interests me. And when I get in my car and turn on the satellite Broadway channel and Seth Rudetsky comes on the air, man, I'm hooked. I'm belting out show tunes while driving (which, thanks to cell phones, doesn't make me look all that crazy anymore). And for no other reason than because this guy Seth lives, breathes, and would eat Broadway if it came in edible form. You can't stop listening to him. He's not only knowledgeable about the smallest facts in a way a true fan is, but he's exhilarated just talking about it. When someone loves something that much, you can't help but be smitten with it, too.

Similarly, I don't consider myself a big fan of the gossip world. I know that Brad and Angelina are still together, but it's not like I can name their kids (they have more than one, right?). Still, I have become addicted to the first fifteen minutes of *The Wendy Williams Show*, when she does her "Hot Topics" segment. Again, it's solely because this is a woman who is consumed. If she were on death row and was offered either a last meal or a chance to yak about the Kardashians, she'd gladly starve so she could yenta it up about the first family of reality TV. I give Wendy Williams a lot of props—when you can make a fan out of someone who registered zero on the interest meter, that's an energy of electric proportion you're putting out there.

Which is another reason I love talking to other funny people so much. I can talk for hours to a stand-up comic or comedy writer whom I've never met, because I'm still endlessly fascinated by the art form. I don't think a day will ever come when I'm "filled up" talking about comedy. Which is one way that I know I made the right decision to pursue stand-up back when I was a college junior and passed the audition at the Comic Strip. This work is where my heart and passion live. I know now that going back to school in Binghamton was never an option. I'd found my life's calling. (Besides, you try braving the winters in upstate New York.)

When I was a kid, I was obsessed with Soupy Sales, he of "Do the Mouse"/pie-in-the-face fame. (Kids, check him out on YouTube.) I thought he was the funniest person I'd ever seen, and I would run home from school to catch his show on channel 5. I constantly wrote fan letters to Soupy and plotzed (remember, this was Long Island) when an autographed postcard from him arrived in our mailbox. I Scotch-taped it to the headboard of my bed until granting it permanent residence in my Peanuts scrapbook.

At some point I read in a fan magazine that Soupy liked to eat at a little Italian joint called Minetta Tavern, on MacDougal Street in Greenwich Village. The article even had pictures of him dining there with his family. And I remember asking my parents if we could go to Minetta Tavern, convinced that when we did, Soupy would be there, too, and I could meet him in person. Well, you don't have to be a genius to figure out that when my parents did take me to eat there, Soupy was a no-show. But I still left that restaurant happy as a clam (an idiom that, given the usual fate of clams in Italian restaurants, seems somewhat less than accurate). The reason, of course, was simple: I was in the place that Soupy went to. We sat at a table where, maybe, Soupy once sat. Ordered from the same menu. I felt close to my idol, and even in that abstract way, it meant everything to me.

This story has so much resonance for me this many years later for another reason. As a kid, I never thought about how amazing it was that my parents actually took me to Minetta Tavern. Especially because it would have been so easy for them to toss the idea away with any number of rationales.

Mom: "Sweetie, the odds of you running into Soupy Sales on a random night are just meshugenah!"

Dad: "The schlep into the city? And then with those Manhattan restaurant prices?"

But they didn't say those things. We got on the train, we schlepped, and my dad paid the inflated New York dinner prices. Because loving me as they did, my parents didn't mind pursuing my pipe dream for a night in the service of supporting my bigger dream—being somehow connected to comedy.

I'm reminded of all this now that I have my own young son with my partner, Lori. And when he displays a particular passion for something, I hope to give him his own Minetta Tavern experience, chasing whatever crazy fan desire he comes up with. Trust me, I'll just be so jazzed that he's fired up about something.

Even if it's baseball. (Seriously. I mean, who knows . . . but this kid does have some arm. Plus, he's from Latin America, and that can't hurt.)

So find the one thing that demands your attention, your own personal Soupy Sales. What is the topic for which the discussion never ends? The subject that could keep a conversation going on a train from New York to Florida, if you met a stranger interested in the same thing? The answer is a good indicator of what career to aim for. (And if you're a parent, have your antennae out to pick up this kind of interest in your kids.)

When you're a fan of the industry you're in, that enthusiasm will inevitably bring you a Barry Levinson moment, when passion for your profession helps you stand out among rivals. And occasionally, you might get a decent Italian meal in Greenwich Village out of it, too.

Soupy's postcard to me. Check out the 4-cent stamp!

# CHAPTER 4

## SO I STOLE SODA FROM AARON SPELLING

In 1987, I was riding a good wave. My stand-up was getting a lot of notice, and my agent asked me to come out from New York to meet with some folks in Los Angeles. I was especially psyched when I heard that one of the execs who wanted to meet with me was the head of Aaron Spelling's production company. At the time, Aaron Spelling was the king of TV, with a ton of shows on the air, among them *Dynasty*, *The Love Boat*, and *Hotel*, and he hoped to branch out into comedy.

So I went over to Aaron Spelling's office with my manager at the time, Tom, and we had a meeting with Spelling's great development guy. This exec was a big fan, had seen a bunch of my late-night spots on *Letterman*, and was excited about the possibility of working together. Tom and I left very pleased—I had a good foot in a very important door.

As we were on our way out, I was feeling really thirsty. We passed a huge refrigerator, tucked into the recess of a hallway. I told Tom I was going to open the fridge to see if there were some drinks inside. Tom immediately cautioned me about doing this.

"Carol, you don't know whose refrigerator that is," he said.

"Tom, I think you're being a little nuts here. It's not like I'm taking something out of a fridge in somebody's office."

"Still, I don't think you should do it."

Thinking Tom was being overly cautious, I opened the refrigerator door, which revealed it was stacked top to bottom with cold sodas. Mind you, no Tupperware labeled "Betty's Egg Salad," nothing partially eaten. No newspaper cartoons or funny magnets stuck to the door, either. I grabbed a Diet Coke and we headed out.

The next day when I was back in New York, I got a frantic call from my agent:

"What the hell happened over at Aaron Spelling's office?!?" Maybe I should have taken a Sprite.

So on the face of it, taking a can of soda from an anonymous refrigerator doesn't seem like the biggest deal breaker. But why take the chance? Something I often tell myself—and anyone else who needs to hear it—is "control what you can and forget about the rest." Avoid a potential problem that's in your power to avoid, no matter how insignificant it may seem. You never know which iceberg—or ice-cold soda—will be the one that capsizes you.

Whatever your profession, we're living in an incredibly competitive time, especially when it comes to hiring. During an interview, you should picture two hundred other candidates competing for the same job, a hundred of whom are younger and hungrier than you are. (Which for some readers will mean going up against twelve-year-olds, but trust me, they're out there.) The other hundred are older and more experienced than you. Plus, throw in a few who went to school with the boss's kid, who know the boss's chiropractor, or who have some other personal connection. I'm not saying this to spook you, only to motivate you to do everything you can to make your best impression.

Over the years, I've gone on a lot of interviews, known a lot of job hunters, and done plenty of hiring myself. And again and again, I've found there are small mistakes people make when looking for a job, mistakes that are incredibly dumb and completely avoidable (did I mention my visit to Aaron Spelling's office?). So here's my Big List of Duh, the stuff that all job seekers, at any level, should know like the back of their resumes. As obvious as some of these may seem, there are plenty of people who commit these crimes against hirability. But now you never will!

### Being Late

This is number one with a bullet, the top vote-getter in the Stupid Job Hunter Hall of Fame. Time management is important—not just with job interviews but with *everything* related to business. When you're prompt to a meeting, you're telling the person that you value them and their time. When you're not, you're telling them that they're just one more thing on your to-do list, like picking up cat food or having your tires rotated. You're asking this person to hire you, for God's sake. Give you a steady paycheck. Help feed you. Being late to the interview is like showing up on a blind date and the first words out of your mouth are "So we're going Dutch tonight, right?" This is the first time you get to show your prospective employer that you can follow instructions and be dependable.

For regular appointments or meetings, I'd say you've got five minutes of wiggle room. But as far as job interviews go, there is no grace period. If you're not ready and available when they call your name, you're losing big points with every passing minute. For my own interviews, I bring a puzzle or a magazine, get there early, and just chill before they ask for me to come in. If you arrive more than five minutes early, do tell the receptionist who you are and that you realize you're a little early. That way they don't wonder "Who's the strange person doing Sudoku on our couch?" If you're super early, maybe grab a coffee across the street until it's ten minutes to meeting time, so you won't come off as a weird creepy lurker hanging around the waiting area.

Look, I'm well aware there are unavoidable intervening factors in life—a flat tire, a broken-down bus or subway, being stopped for a ticket. In my experience, those really unavoidable reasons happen about one percent of the time. The other ninety-nine percent, lateness boils down to bad planning ("I couldn't decide which top to wear" or "I wanted to see who won on this *Judge Judy* episode I was watching"). If that dreaded one percent does happen to you—once, the electric gate of the parking garage in my apartment building wouldn't open, holding me hostage for two hours—be prepared. Do you know the office number so you can call and tell them you're trapped in a canyon with your arm pinned under a boulder? Is it better to get in touch with them by text or e-mail? Know this info in advance so you can act before you black out.

As an aside, here's a little phenomenon I've noticed every time I've been in hiring mode: a prospective hire comes in late as an unspoken power play. As if to say, "Yeah, I know you're important and everything, but guess what, *I am, too.*" And they always feel the need to mention whatever important event kept them from being on time. Don't be that person. Be the person who wants the job so badly that you followed the one big demand: to arrive at the appointed time. You're controlling something you can control, your own promptness, the first step to making a good impression.

## Questionable Hygiene

Unfortunately, more people need help with this problem than you'd think.

First let me address my male readers, because I think you need special attention when it comes to this subject. I'm going to throw out two facts that you'd think most guys would already know, but not all of them do. So listen up, fellows.

**Hygiene Fact One:** WHEN YOU HAVE A JOB INTERVIEW, YOU NEED TO TAKE A SHOWER BEFOREHAND. Not a week before, not the night before, but *the morning of the interview*. And not a quick rinse-off but a real shower, one that includes soap (from a store) and lots of scrubbing. Pretend you just finished running a marathon. Maybe two.

**Hygiene Fact Two:** IF YOU APPLY AFTERSHAVE OR COLOGNE AFTER SAID SHOWER, YOU MUST USE IT *SPARINGLY*. It's not a flea dip, guys. In fact, I'd say toss the cologne completely. Except for a handful of gay guys, I've never known a man who smells *better* with aftershave on. The benefit of a good hearty shower is that you smell naturally clean afterward.

Hey, didn't mean to freak you out with the caps and italics above. I just want to be sure I get this point across! I can't tell you how many times I've interviewed guys who walked into my office and their funk walked in right after them—so much that I thought I was going to have to offer it its own chair. It's incredibly distracting. Many times I'm sitting there trying to figure out what exactly is that combo in the funk. Like, "Is that Funyuns mixed with a pack of Newports?" "Can moth balls actually eat a Whopper?"

Or sometimes a guy's gross cologne gets all over my hand when we shake. Nothing worse than stinking and then spreading it. When that happens, I can't concentrate at all—I'm counting the minutes until the interview is over and I can wash it off, so I don't smell like I got maced with a bottle of Hai Karate. So, shower! And leave the cologne for your brother and the girl he met on Plenty of Fish.

This cologne thing now segues over to women. Gals, heed the advice I just gave to the men: less is more. You're trying to get a job, not get hired by an escort service. So go easy on the perfume. Same for the makeup and jewelry. When in doubt, always side with "subtle."

And ladies, for God's sake get a manicure before you interview, even if it's a no-polish one. Nothing worse than looking across a desk and seeing someone's chewed-up funky-ass nails.

Which leads to the subject of how to dress for a job interview . . .

## What Not to Wear

Unlike the common-sense topic of time management, navigating this one requires a little more thought. I guess my standard advice would be to dress the part. If you're interviewing in a law office, you'd wear a suit. If you're interviewing to be a bike messenger, a suit would be weird. So figure out the environment of the place you're attempting to gain employment at and match it. When in doubt, dress a shade up rather than a shade down. (When I do stand-up, I always aim to dress one degree fancier than the audience. To me, it's a respect thing. Like, "You've taken the time to buy a ticket to come see my little show, so let me dress up a little more than maybe you have.")

This is an area where I'd like to address women in particular. Five-inch stiletto heels are a great choice, gals, if you're interviewing to be a stripper. In fact, maybe that's all you'd need. But it's not such a good idea for a receptionist at a podiatrist's office. This may sound weird, but even in an office setting, the person who does the hiring will want to know that you won't be hampered because you decided to wear stilts on your feet. Which is not to say that you need to interview in a pair of running shoes (clerk at Foot Locker being the obvious exception). Sensible footwear, please.

The same goes with clothes that are too sexy. I've seen women come in for interviews who apparently felt it necessary to show off their incredible rack in a low-cut top. Sorry, but putting your best cup forward is a bad choice. You're at a job interview, not spring break in Cancun. So save the super-sexy outfits for the club and the boob men lining the bar.

Last point: Man or woman, you don't need to break the bank on interview outfits. Plenty of midpriced stores are more than able to supply you with professional-looking choices (although who in their right mind would ever shop at a place called Dress Barn?). If there's one area where you might splurge, I would recommend getting a good haircut. I've seen people transform their entire look just by finding a top-notch stylist. There's no bigger turnoff than someone in a Brooks Brothers suit with a Moe-from-the-Three-Stooges haircut.

Being on time, looking nice, not smelling like the trash bin behind a Korean barbecue joint . . . that's a good start, but it's only a start. There are still plenty of ways to screw up once your meeting gets under way. So keep reading.

## Come On In!

"You never get a second chance to make a first impression." I know that line comes from an old Head & Shoulders commercial, but I wish I'd thought of it. Because it's true (more so than "Gee Your Hair Smells Terrific").

To make that great first impression, the first thing to do—even before entering the room—is to make sure your *phone is off.* Nothing brings an interview to a grinding halt like a Black Eyed Peas ringtone belting out from the middle of nowhere. That would annoy even Fergie.

Next up, watch your handshake. It's such a bummer when you immediately like someone, then you shake hands and it all falls apart. A problem handshake usually falls into one of two polar-opposite categories: the limp fish or the death grip of Thor. I think this is an area where men have a bit of an advantage—they've been more socialized to shake hands. So if you're a woman and feel a little awkward when you shake, practice with someone until you can reliably deliver a firm but not finger-crushing grip. Develop the habit of looking the person in the eye when you shake, too. It's a small but important detail. (Note: Avoid fist bumps, high-fives, one-arm man hugs—anything you might have seen when guys greet each other in beer commercials.)

I've always found that an intimidating part of the interview is deciding where to sit, especially if your seat's not obvious, like a lone chair in front of someone's desk, or if you're meeting with multiple people. That's why as we're walking in I always ask, "Where would you like me to sit?" This way, there's not that awkward little dance, and you don't make the dreaded mistake of taking somebody else's "spot." People can be very territorial about seating arrangements. (Just think back to Dad's Barcalounger in the den.)

## It's an Interview, Not a Starbucks

Your energy level is crucial during a job interview. Sitting forward, being connected and "up" indicate that you're a good candidate. It's really annoying when the person you're interviewing sits like he or she is lazily enjoying a fourth latte of the day (or in a guy's case, a sixth hour of playing *Call of Duty*). Conversely, don't be so manic that you're bouncing off the walls. No one wants to feel like the office has suddenly become a Chuck E. Cheese restaurant. (What does that middle initial stand for, anyway?) Just be an engaged and positive presence.

Cursing is a shockingly common misstep. It's a behavior that definitely falls into the category of "I don't need to do this, it could be damaging, so why do it?" It isn't simply a matter of someone being a conservative prude. Your interviewer may be thinking, "If I hire you, is this how you'll speak to clients?" Too risky! F-bomb all you want when it's your personal time, but when you're in somebody's office, act like it's primetime on the networks and the FCC has its lawyers on speed dial.

And guys? Never call a woman "ma'am," no matter how respectful you think it is. Replace the word with "incontinent old bag" and you'll get an idea of what it feels like.

## But Enough about Me—What Do *You* Think about Me?

Another rookie mistake I've made while interviewing was talking endlessly about myself. This is an occupational hazard for comics, but it's a trap anyone can fall into. Yes, showcasing yourself is a key element of scoring a job, but it's always good to remember that even interviews are *conversations*. Be present and aware that you're talking with someone else who has likes and interests. It's a good idea to do an Internet search on the person (and company) you're meeting to find out more about him, her, or them— hobbies, charitable endeavors, etc. For example, I am way into animal rescue. It's my passion. This information is all over my Wikipedia page and many press pieces. So if I was interviewing someone and they told me that they volunteer at a shelter, or love the work of the Humane Society, or had a rescue dog, that would give them a leg up (sorry) in my book. Fair or not, that's just the way it is.

In most meetings, you'll hear the dreaded phrase: "Do you

have any questions for *me*?" It's usually toward the end, and it always catches you off guard, as if you were suddenly asked, "Who's your favorite boy band?" ("Don't make me choose!" I would say desperately, and then sob uncontrollably.) So prepare for it. Even if it's something as simple as, "Yes, I do have a question. What are you looking for with this hire that you didn't find before?" Or just go with a simple, friendly "When did you join the company?" I've found that people always like to share their own job histories, so deploying that question is a safe bet.

## Be Good to the Gatekeepers

Most people you interview with will have an assistant or a secretary. *Be really nice to those people.* These gatekeepers often have input into the hiring discussion. Say the boss comes out of her office after you've left and remarks, "I really liked that person. I think she's my top pick so far." And then the assistant says, "Well, she left her empty energy drink can on the coffee table for me to clean up and never returned the key to the can after being in there for half an hour." Suddenly, you're sunk.

So you want to leave that assistant with something nice to say about you, or at least not give him reasons to "accidentally" delete your contact info. Besides, if you're lucky enough to get hired, an assistant who likes you can be tremendously helpful in navigating the tricky landscape of your new workplace. I'm not saying to be such a blatant kiss-ass that you show up to your interview with flowers and truffles for the receptionist. But it's extremely important to see the office as a full environment, not just one lone boss in a vacuum. You want to make a good impression on everyone you encounter.

## Know Your ABCs

It's not as if anyone gives you a pop English quiz when you sit down for a job interview. But any correspondence with your prospective employer is going to be part of the mix, which is why it's so important to use correct grammar and spelling in e-mails and letters. It looks bad when someone doesn't take the time to write correctly, especially when the information for proper usage is out there and easily available. (Hello, spellcheck!) Any mistakes you make are recorded in print, or the digital equivalent. As they used to threaten in school, it becomes part of your permanent record.

I'm particularly sensitive to this point, since my last name is a tricky one to spell. It violates the old adage of "i before e, except after c." I can't tell you how many times I receive requests in a letter or e-mail with "Leifer" spelled incorrectly. Or even my first name—they'll add an "e" to the end of "Carol." Oh, the horrors! But to be honest, it's an immediate turnoff. I figure, if this person couldn't take the two seconds to google me and learn the right way to spell my name, why should I consider the request? Taking the time to be certain your correspondence is properly spelled—including (especially) the name of the person you're communicating with—is a good example of attending to a simple but important aspect of the hiring process that's under your control. No doubt there's someone else out there up for the same job who has stellar spelling and grammar.

## Keep It Short and Sweet

Another priority for e-mails and letters is to keep them brief. (But don't be cute about it. Spell out the words, even in e-mail. K? GR8.) When someone I don't know sends me a message and it's l-o-o-o-n-g, I usually delete it. Always remember the importance and value of someone else's time. It took me many years to learn that people who are successful are overwhelmingly busy. They've got a lot going on and their attention is at a premium. So if you hope to catch just a small portion of it, you've got to be quick, clear, and succinct.

Being able to do so not only means that your correspondence is more likely to be read, it also shows that you know how to zero in on what's important. Being able to distill concepts to their essential elements is a hugely important skill in business. Your message should not be so lengthy and overwritten that it reads like a summary of the company's 401(k). Twitter has the right idea, and I feel it's a key to the company's success—whatever you want to say, try to communicate it in fewer than 140 characters.

And speaking of Facebook and Twitter and all the other

social media sites out there, DON'T POST ANYTHING THAT YOU WOULDN'T WANT A POTENTIAL EMPLOYER TO SEE. PLENTY OF COMPANIES CHECK OUT YOUR PROFILE, AND AS *BIG BROTHER* (NOVEL, NOT CBS REALITY SHOW) AS THAT IS, IT'S A REALITY. I LOVE THAT YOU WON A FIERCE ROUND OF BEER PONG, BUT DON'T GO SHOWING THE WORLD.

(SIDENOTE: MY BEST FRIEND'S DAUGHTER WAS FIRED FROM HER WAITRESSING JOB BECAUSE OF A BAD YELP REVIEW THAT NAMED HER. IT'S A DRAG, COMPLETELY NOT FAIR, BUT THAT'S THE WAY IT IS.)

Sorry about the caps again, but by now you know how I am.

## Plan Your Sequel

It's a good rule of thumb to always send a thank-you note after an interview. Not an e-mail, mind you, but the old reliable hand-written message on nice stationery. You have the address—you interviewed there—or you can get it off the business card (the one you should always ask for as you're leaving the interview).

Again, make the note short and sweet. As simple as "Dear ____. Thank you for taking the time to meet with me. I hope I have the opportunity to work with you—if not now, then sometime in the future. Best regards, ____." Anyone would like to receive a note like that (assuming you fill in the ____s with the correct names).

## Give Yourself a Break

Hopefully, following all this advice will help you feel more confident when they call your name and you walk into that office. But remember, everybody's nervous when they go after a job. Even after many years in the business, I still won't drink a cup of coffee before an interview, because I know my heart will be racing already.

If you're at the beginning of your career path, know that the beauty of interviewing is that, like everything else, with practice it becomes easier. Even enjoyable, as strange as that may sound to entry-level novices. I may get nervous, but I love meeting new people and checking out places I've never been before. When I'm on an interview, I try not to focus on whether I'll be hired. I just want to be the best "me" I can. Then I'll have no regrets if I don't wind up with the gig. AND I HOPE YOU STRIVE TO DO THE SAME.

Okay, now I'm just being obnoxious with the caps.

Me and Tubby—what a bill!

# CHAPTER 5

## SPIELBERG WASN'T AVAILABLE

I like watching morning news shows when I wake up; it's my habit. One particular morning, on one of my favorite morning shows, the hosts teased that a group of women (among them Trudie Styler and Gwyneth Paltrow) was going to be promoting short films they directed for *Glamour* magazine, a series called "Reel Moments." I was intrigued because I, too, have always dreamed of directing a short film. The interview came on and I immediately fell in love with the idea—short films inspired by women (*Glamour* readers), shot by women (the celebs). I thought the "celeb" part might knock me out of the running if I pursued trying to participate in the series. But then they mentioned that one of the directors was a writer colleague of mine, the talented Jenny Bicks of *Sex and the City* fame, so I figured maybe I had a shot.

I called my agent to find out if they were doing another round. She got back to me quickly, saying that the production house, Moxie Pictures, was in preproduction for another set of films. The bad news: they had already secured all the talent. Now, for many people, that might be where the story ends. But not for me. I was like a dog with a bone!

I asked my agent to please relay my disappointment that no spots were open at that time but to see if, the next time I was in New York, I could have a general meeting with the production house. My agent followed through (yes, that sometimes happens) and the execs were open to it.

Cut to two months later, and I'm in New York. I sat down with the folks at Moxie Pictures and we had a nice easy-breezy confab. I told them how bummed I was that I didn't get the opportunity to take part in the *Glamour* series, but that I hoped they would think of me in the future. Now, even at this point in the story, some might still call it a bust, right?

Well, three months after that, I got a call. The directors of one of the shorts had dropped out, having gotten staff jobs on a television show. And guess who Moxie thought of to replace them? Sofia Coppola, but she was tipsy at her uncle's winery, so unavailable. No, just fibbing. They asked me!

I went on to direct a short film called *Blinders*. We cast Jamie Lyn Sigler, of *Sopranos* fame, for the female lead, and, I'm very proud to say now, a then-unknown actor named Matthew Morrison (of *Glee*) as the male lead. Both super-cool people, by the way. Directing a film turned out to be everything I had dreamed of, although I skipped wearing the requisite baseball cap because of "hat hair" concerns. As someone who started her career in New York City, I was thrilled to shoot in Manhattan.

One of the "pinch me!" moments of my career.
(There's "Jen," second from right.)

They closed city streets for us, and we even got to film on an IRT subway. All my fantasies of being a female Woody Allen fulfilled! (Minus marrying my stepdaughter.)

The other directors in the *Glamour* series were Bryce Dallas Howard, Andrea Buchanan, and Jennifer Aniston. Jennifer, being a good friend of Oprah Winfrey, told us that she'd spoken personally to Ms. O, who relayed that she was dying to have us *all* on her show to promote the films. Woo-hoo!

When the time came to tape the show, Jen (do you like how after only two sentences I've started calling her "Jen"?) raised the experience to a whole new stupendous level by inviting us to fly to Chicago on her private jet. I would have been excited even if she'd asked me to be the flight attendant. The show couldn't have gone better. Oprah even commented on how much she loved particular moments of my short, which made a permanent deposit in the old memory bank.

But as I've often mentioned throughout this book, yours truly is a connector, *big time*, and I left Chicago with budding friendships with many of Oprah's producers. I genuinely like getting to know people when I work someplace new. But in any situation, the business part of yourself always needs to be engaged, connecting, and thinking forward. It's not a question of using people (which is frowned upon in show business, of course). It's just that you should never leave a work experience without a ton of business cards or new contacts added to your phone. And afterward, don't forget these people—stay in touch. Which I did, with an e-mail here and a note there to comment on a particular Oprah episode that I'd seen and liked, adding them all to my holiday card list, and so on.

So it should be no surprise that when my first book came out three years later, getting on *Oprah* to promote it was well within my reach. That's not to say it was easy—when Oprah was on network TV, every author and their mother (mine, no exception) knew that getting on that show was the shortest route to the best-seller list. But my contacts with Oprah's people were deep, and I started from a distinct advantage, working diligently until my publicist and I, in tandem, got a "yes!"

And it all started with a meeting for a project that had already been staffed. So whatever job you're in or aspire to get, you'll never go wrong sharing your genuine enthusiasm with those involved and keeping tabs with folks you meet as you pursue your goals. When you have your heart set on an opportunity that slips from your grasp, forming a connection to the people who can make it possible is the next best thing. Especially when you witness that happy accident, a seemingly missed chance that does a complete one-hundred-eighty-degree turn.

Tenacity will always make you a winner. Though the odds of ending up on a private jet with Jennifer Aniston (I mean, Jen) . . . still very small.

# CHAPTER 6

## THE RULE OF TEN

I've always had a pretty simple philosophy about business—I like to treat people the way I'd like to be treated. That's not to say I'm not tough and a mo-fo when I have to be. But overall, it doesn't take much to be a kind and giving person. And as far as your career is concerned, as you'll find out down the road, it's smart to be nice.

This many years into my work journey, I get the occasional pleasant reminder about having been a good egg here and there along the way. There's a great comedy writer named Gary Janetti, of *Family Guy* and *Will & Grace* fame, whom I've worked with over the years. When we were first introduced, it made me laugh when Gary surprised me by saying that we had already met. In the early 1990s I was headlining at Caroline's in New York City and staying at the Paramount hotel. Gary was the front desk clerk who checked me in, and apparently he'd told me that he was a big fan. So I gave him a couple of comp tickets to go see my show, and then I requested fresh towels every six hours. (Okay, I made that last part up.)

It seems that I have also been pleasant to waitresses who were aspiring actresses at one time. Megyn Price, who starred in the CBS show *Rules of Engagement*, for which I was a writer/producer, told me that she had worked the take-out counter of Maria's Italian Kitchen in L.A. when she was struggling to make it in show business. She said that I was always friendly to her when I went in to pick up food. She still remembers the tips I put in the jar on the counter. (But thankfully not all the extra napkins and plasticware I took.) Same thing with Kate Flannery of *The Office*. When I met her at the Emmys in 2012, she said that she used to wait on me at Kate Mantilini (still one of my

Callie Khouri, me, and writer Marjorie Gross (may she rest in peace).

favorite restaurants—try the Life Rice!) and that I was always a considerate customer.

These comments from people whose work I admire always makes me feel so good that (a) unchecked I wasn't a surly bastard and (b) they didn't forget it all these years later. If I had been a prick to these people, they sure would have remembered that, too.

I'm still grateful for the incredible gifts of kindness that others have bestowed upon me and my colleagues. The second season that I worked on *Seinfeld* as a writer/producer, I cowrote an episode with the brilliant Marjorie Gross called

With Bette Midler and Marge Gross on the *Seinfeld* set while taping "The Understudy."

"The Understudy." (It's the episode where George and Jerry are suspected of deliberately injuring Bette Midler during a softball game so that Jerry's girlfriend, Bette's understudy, could have a chance to go onstage. At the end, Kramer makes Bette a "Macaroni Midler!") Back then, *Seinfeld* was not the ratings megahit it was to become. We were having a hard time convincing a big-time celebrity to commit to the part. As hard as that is to believe now, every A-list actress was turning us down, including Liza Minnelli, whom I personally pleaded with on the phone to take the role.

The only actress who eventually said yes was Bette Midler, and here's the reason. At that time, Marjorie was battling ovarian cancer. As her bosses, Jerry and Larry could not have been more supportive through Marge's health crisis, letting her rest and take breaks when she needed to, even putting a cot in her office for that very purpose. Bette came through simply because she was an old friend; on hearing about Marge's illness, Bette rallied, wanting to do anything she could for her pal. I even remember Bette changing her tour schedule to tape the episode.

No surprise, Bette went on to be brilliant on *Seinfeld* (I'm still kicking myself that we didn't submit her for a guest actress Emmy nomination). But more important, it showed the kind of heart Bette Midler has. Tragically, Marge passed away a year later from cancer, but that Bette episode was truly a highlight for her.

With Jay Leno in the green room of *Late Night with David Letterman.*

The nicest celebrity I've ever known is Jay Leno, the host they kept rewarding for ruling late night by replacing him. I've never seen Jay pass up an opportunity to take a photo with a fan or give an autograph when someone asks. He used to call it "The Rule of Ten." When you're nice to somebody, they'll go back and tell ten people about their experience with you. Word gets around when you're nice. But the phenomenon is an equal-opportunity employer. It also gets around when you're a rude douche; that intel goes "Rule of Ten," too.

So even if it's not in your nature to be nice, think about it strategically. When I was coming up, I once went to a studio where they made demo reels, or a compilation of TV appearances. It was, and is, a great tool to send around a video of your best stuff. For my reel, I worked closely with an editor named Grant Heslov, who went on to become George Clooney's producing partner and win several Academy Awards. Needless to say, Grant is a major player now. And when we run into each other, I enjoy ribbing him about our "creative collaboration" from way back when. But suppose I had a feature project that I wanted to pitch to him. Wouldn't it suck if I had been a tool when we worked together, and he remembered that? It would be hard to even get in the door to see him.

There's another interesting person I knew from a long time ago, a woman who was a waitress when I was performing at the Improv in L.A. in the mid-1980s. Her name is Callie

Khouri, and she went on to win an Academy Award for writing *Thelma & Louise*. She's currently the executive producer and creator of the ABC drama *Nashville*. I wouldn't mind being interviewed for a staff job at that show one day, so thank the good Lord I wasn't a comic who was a real creep to waitresses. Because there were plenty of those. I love so many of the comics I've met over the years, but there are others who treated the waitstaff like inmates, yelling at them, refusing to call them by their names, displaying all the qualities that eventually made them the lonely, self-loathing middle-aged ex-comics they turned out to be.

So, right from the beginning, make it a habit to be kind. In the techno-world we live in, it's super important because the nasty stuff can trip you up real quick. Particularly with e-mail. I often get e-mail messages that make me mental, sent by people who are being real jackasses in any number of ways. I've made that dreadful mistake of replying right away, with all the vitriol fresh on my fingers and spilling all over the keyboard. Because of those situations, I've made a firm rule for myself. When an e-mail gets me hopped up, I wait twenty-four hours before responding. (Speaking of e-mails, a note to Kohl's: You can stop sending them to me. I know you're having a sale. You're always having a sale.)

No harm, no foul, right? It's always acceptable business etiquette to respond a day later to an e-mail. But more important, during that twenty-four-hour period I've cooled down and am able to send a less emotional response, using words that spellcheck knows. Oh, how I wished I'd made that rule for myself earlier in the game.

So, "be nice." Turns out your mom wasn't so clueless after all. On the other hand, "eat your vegetables" . . . well, I still have a problem with that one, and I'm a vegetarian.

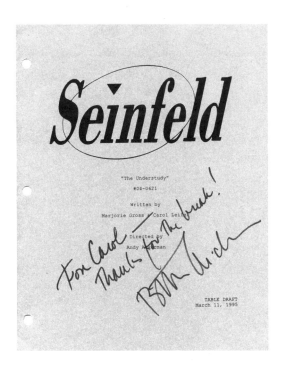

Party at my pad in 1983. (That's Jay's wife, Mavis, in the middle.)

# CHAPTER 7

## BAD VIBRATIONS

My least favorite class in school was gym. Ugh, who had the patience for it, especially in the middle of the day? Putting on a red "skort" (one of the earliest uses of this fashion nightmare) and then spending the entire next period smelly and sticking to the back of your chair?

Even worse was being sent to the school psychologist. You knew you were a certifiable whack job if you had to take a walk down that lonely hall to the man in the argyle vest smoking a pipe. And yet looking back, those experiences, ironically, provided two of the most important takeaways from my education: Keep your mind resilient. Keep your body strong.

Because any business endeavor is a challenge. To stay at the top of your game, you've got to take care of yourself, mentally and physically. In terms of your psyche—whether an argyle vest is involved or not—strong coping mechanisms are essential for dealing with the inevitable vicissitudes on the roller coaster ride that is your career. (Note to my freshman English teacher: I not only spelled "vicissitudes" correctly, but I used it in a sentence, too.) I hope I'm giving you plenty of strategies throughout this book that will help your mental health, and I'll return to the topic later in this chapter.

On the skort side of things, moving your ass is highly underrated, for both mind and body. You look good as a result of regular exercise, but more important, it keeps your head in the right place. As a writer, I find that connecting to my body via exercise has become the essential counterpart to spending so much time inside my brain. When I'm pent up, angry, or frustrated—all of which consume a startling amount of my time—nothing sweeps the streets of my head like a good spin class. Even driving to the class is relaxing.

I practically live at a place called Blazing Saddles in Sherman Oaks, California. (Check it out. But if you like it, please don't crowd up my morning class.) When I'm on that bike, I think of everything that's making me ballistic; I stare it down and run it over. It's like road rage, except no one gets hurt, just slightly toned. The best part is that, many times when it's a really fierce workout, I'll find solace in knowing that this will probably be the toughest part of my day. (Let's remember that I deal with jokes, not plutonium.)

So learn to love to sweat, and try to learn it early in life. If you never exercise, the last thing you want to hear from a doctor when you're forty is "You better start." (Actually, that's the second-to-last thing you want to hear from a doctor.) If you wait until middle age to try to get into shape, you might find yourself exhausted just from shopping for workout gear (even if you're doing it online).

Working out, of course, helps you keep the weight off (should bookstores shelve this book in the "Health and Fitness" section?). Personally, I am fanatic about staying trim. I'm even a lifetime member of Weight Watchers (you'd think they'd send me a cake or something, but no). And I'm fanatic because I discovered that absolutely no good comes from being heavy. Even people who get on televised weight-loss shows can't be too happy they got the gig. ("Hey, Mom! Hear the good news? I'm so obese that I'm going to be on a TV show where people yell at me because I'm fat, and every week they put me on a scale used to weigh livestock. Mom? You there . . . ?")

In the late eighties I let myself go, weighing in at one hundred and fifty-nine pounds (oh, the relief of not hitting one-six-o on that scale!). And it was nothing short of a nightmare, the six months I lumbered around at that tonnage. It culminated one night at the Improv, where I removed my sweater midset and a heckler yelled out from the audience, "Sooie!!!!!" It was one of my worst moments ever as a stand-up, and I've got quite the Rolodex of "worst moments" to choose from.

In fact, pardon this slight detour to hear about my *actual* worst moment as a stand-up comic. After my third appearance on *Late Night with David Letterman* in 1982, my agent got a call from one of the Beach Boys, the late Carl Wilson, asking if I could open for the group at Harrah's Casino in Lake Tahoe over Christmas week. I was, naturally, thrilled to get this opportunity. Unfortunately, I was a little too green for the opponent that is a casino crowd. Needless to say—but I'll say it—the gig was a nightmare. First off, the ever-polite and professional Beach Boys would tune up during my set. Not having an agent or manager with me on the gig, I had to be the fun agent of change, asking them timidly if they could stop doing that. (They didn't.) Then, at the New Year's Eve show, I got a table right up front crowded with drunk frat-house boys. Not only did they chant "Reefer! Reefer!" during the first five minutes of my set (mocking my last name . . . good one, college boys), but they followed up by pulling on my microphone cord as if it was a fishing line. Absolutely no one from the casino was policing the room, which left me to desperately pull back on the cord as if I were Papa Hemingway and the frat house boys a group of marlin. This memory still has the power to wake me up in the middle of the night in a cold, panicky sweat.

But getting back to our discussion of flab . . .

At this stage in my career, nothing spells "old" like becoming a big pot-bellied lug. I'm committed to keeping my weight down simply because so many of my contemporaries have just said "screw it" and let the pounds roll on. It's depressing.

I'm not, of course, belittling obesity or its effects. (Well, minimally I am.) For many people, being overweight is a lifelong struggle over which they have little control. But there are others, myself included, who are not in that group. And I've seen more than a few of them—us—give up, become lazy. It's like they're saying, "You win, world!" To me, that attitude communicates "I don't care much about myself. So how much am I going to care about this job?" (Depends on what kind of vending machines they've got in the office, I guess.)

Similarly, I still have friends who don't get annual checkups. They avoid going to a doctor for many reasons—usually because they're scared of what they might find out. Or maybe they already have a lot of old magazines at home and don't feel a particular need to go to some office to read a bunch more. Whatever the reason, these folks don't get checkups, and eventually they don't need to. It's crazy. They wind up with a diagnosis of cancer or some other horrible disease that could have been caught early; they might have been able to save their lives if they had just done the whole nine yards with a routine physical. So do yourself the biggest favor ever and go see the good doc—one who has diplomas on the wall and plastic models of body parts you can play with when no one is in the room. Sure, it's embarrassing to be asked gross and personal questions. But always remember that "dying from embarrassment" is just an expression.

Now let's return to the subject of your head, the body part in use right now (I hope) as you read my book. First, let me come right out and say it: I highly encourage you to go into therapy.

And I say that without even meeting you, because I don't have to. Trust me, you've got problems. Everybody does. I've been in therapy for most of my adult life, still valiantly trying to work out my problems in the proper location of a board-certified shrink's office. Because if I've seen anything over the course of my career, it's that people who've never dealt with their issues will take them out somewhere along the work road, where they don't belong. To staggeringly self-sabotaging results.

But I'm fair. If it's not therapy, then just find someplace safe where you can work on your problems, as long as it's legal and doesn't hurt anyone else.

I'm also a big fan of journaling. I've found it very useful to always track my goals and expectations so there's a reality gauge on paper. When everything's down in black and white, you'll have visible evidence of what eventually drove you to drink.

The biggest recent change in my life came when I started practicing transcendental meditation (TM), which I had assumed was something for old hippies or Beatles. But my friend Jerry Seinfeld, who is neither of those things, has been an ardent enthusiast of TM for as long as I've known him. In 2009, I accompanied him to a Change Begins Within benefit concert at Radio City Music Hall, an event to raise funds for the teaching of TM to at-risk youths, veterans, and other groups. Jerry performed (and killed, natch), and the benefit got me interested.

Now, we all know that when you attend an event that's

dedicated to lauding something, it's hard to leave without being affected by it, even if it's an Herbalife seminar. But something really connected with me that night about TM—mostly the testimonials of people who shared how it had completely changed their life. Howard Stern and his wife, Beth, were there. (That's three name drops in two paragraphs, for those of you counting.) And being a longtime fan of his show, I knew what a TM fan Howard was.

So when I hung out that summer with Howard and Beth (yes, I'm "hung-dropping" now), I mentioned how I was intrigued by TM but intimidated by the idea of learning it. Coincidentally, Beth had just learned the basics a day or two earlier. Upon hearing how quickly she was able to pick it up, I was no longer so overwhelmed by the concept. When I got back to L.A., my partner, Lori, and I took the TM introductory class, and the technique was as easy and natural as promised. (Interested? I'll give you the simple, exact advice that Howard gave me: "Go to TM.org." That's literally all you need to know to get started.)

TM has had a profound effect on my life these past few years. I am a much calmer, more centered, happier person. Any stress that's thrown my way, I can now disassemble it so much more effectively. And I sleep like a friggin' baby (that's first use of the phrase "friggin' baby" in any publication that I know of). I used to need a lot of sleep meds to get through my crazy schedule traveling to gigs, but I don't need any now. Plus, doing TM has really freed up my creativity. (Maybe that's not evident from this chapter, but it's true.) I know I'm starting to sound a bit like a snake oil salesman, but as far as I'm concerned, TM is truly a miracle waiting inside everyone. Did I mention TM.org?

Whether or not you try TM, or therapy, or a spinning class, or some other method, the point is this: Take care of yourself. When you work at keeping your mind and body in shape, you're sharpening the best tools in your career arsenal. And if, like me, you have unpleasant memories of high school gym class, find strength in knowing that the skort need never be part of future employment endeavors.

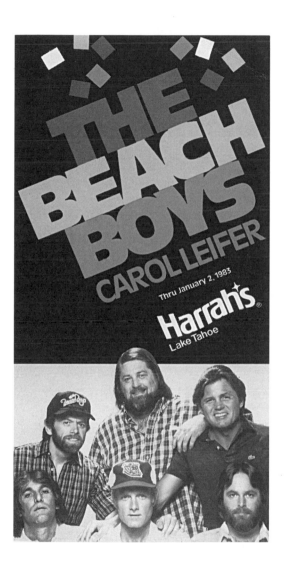

# CHAPTER 8

## I'M HARRY DEAN STANTON'S MOMMY

My partner, Lori, and I are sitting at a Simon and Garfunkel reunion concert, anxiously waiting for the show to begin.

We're at the Staples Center in Los Angeles, and we have amazing seats, one of the perks of being with a big talent agency. Your rep might not be great at getting you work, but pick a concert with hard-to-get tickets and you're in! (Believe me, I stayed at my last agency a few years longer than I should have because of said bonus.)

As we're sipping a couple of beers, Lori looks behind us at and says, "Hey! Isn't that Harry Dean Stanton over there? And isn't he sitting with Jack Nicholson?!" I turn around to see that Lori was indeed right. Wow! We've got even better seats than they do.

Then Lori says, "Why don't you go over to Harry Dean Stanton and say hi? Didn't you have dinner with him and a bunch of other people not too long ago?" My partner, who has the memory of an elephant, was very much correct (as you can see from the opposite page). I did share a great night with Harry Dean Stanton and a bunch of comedian friends at the Palm Restaurant. Richard Belzer is a good friend of Harry Dean's, and he invited some comics and comedy writers (among them Dom Irrera, Jim Vallely, and Jonathan Schmock, who used to make up the comedy team called the Funny Boys). As I recall, a lot of alcohol was consumed that night and we had a pretty rollicking good time. The dinner lasted easily three hours. I'm usually the lone female at these comedian dinners, so at some point in the evening, it's de rigueur that I get an extra-special dose of attention. And if memory serves me correctly, the spotlight on me that evening was a rousing chant of "Mommy! Mommy!" that serenaded me as I downed a shot of tequila.

(My nickname among my comedian pals is "Mommy." As in, Ronald Reagan calling his wife, Nancy, "Mommy." I'm not exactly sure how I got it, but it's stuck for a million years now.)

Back to the Staples Center: "No way," I said to Lori. "I'm not going over there. Especially because Jack Nicholson's sitting over there, too!"

"But what do you always tell me when we go out?" Lori shot back.

I wanted to dodge her question, even though I already knew the answer. Sheepishly I confessed and said, "I always tell you to tell me to go over and say hi to people."

Busted!

As much as I didn't want to take the trek back to Harry Dean—and Jake Gittes from *Chinatown*—Lori was correct. I've never gone wrong over the course of my career by going out of my way to say hello to people, not just close friends, colleagues, and acquaintances but even people I barely know. True, if you're not a natural glad-hander—or maybe if you're just not in the mood—it can be hard to muster the courage and approach someone you don't know well. But even if it's never fun doing it, it's always the smart thing to do. I've found that some really cool things can come from just casually running into someone in a social setting.

That fact fired up my chutzpah. Yeah! I thought to myself. It'd be stupid *not* to say something to Harry Dean. For God's sake, we broke three kinds of expensive bread together! He called me Mommy in a group setting!

So, I got up.

And I strolled over to Harry Dean (and Jack), keeping my demeanor very up and positive. (I've learned that if you approach celebrities in a meek and mild manner, you'll have a security person in your face in no time.)

"Hey, Harry Dean!" I said. Then, pointing to myself, "It's Carol Leifer. Richard Belzer's buddy?"

A blank stare from Harry Dean greeted me back. But I was not to be deterred, so I went on to elaborate.

"We ate at the Palm recently? Bunch of comedians, with Belzer and you?"

Harry Dean just shook his head no. And not in a searching, friendly way, I might add. More in a can-you-get-the-hell-outta-here, I'm-with-Jack-Nicholson way. I should also say at this point that if Jack Nicholson were ever given the role of the Sphinx, he would crush it. The man, behind his requisite sunglasses, did not even swivel his head one degree to acknowledge my presence in any way.

I was stuck.

In these socially awkward situations, you find yourself relying purely on the moment to tell you what to do. And for some strange reason, my moment told me to stay there. And dig myself into an even bigger hole than I already had.

I marched on valiantly.

"We were all drinking a lot and telling jokes and stories, and . . ." I practically listed what each of us had ordered that night. "You had the T-bone and I had the chopped Italian salad with a side of broccoli rabe?" Nothing was breaking this guy. And so I just kept babbling like a mental patient, "It was a Wednesday night, so the valet parking wasn't all that jammed up . . ." I was like someone with Tourette's, except I kept it all clean.

At some point, though, I had to admit defeat. Any nearby usher could have told me that. So after probably mentioning all the specific types of bread that had graced the bread basket at the dinner table, I put an end to it. I simply said, "Well anyway, Harry Dean, I thought I'd just come by and say hi. Enjoy the concert."

I turned around and embarked on the long walk of shame back to my seat. I could see in the distance that Lori's head was bowed—even from that far away, I'm sure she experienced some of the peripheral frostiness from the encounter.

Then, after I had walked about ten rows, I heard a voice shouting loudly: "I REMEMBER NOW!!" I turned back around to see it was Harry Dean, now standing up and yelling to me. I gave Harry and the Sphinx an acknowledging wave and settled back into my seat while paging the beer guy for another extra-large brew.

Whew. Believe it or not, the moral of this story is *still* that you should always say hi and be sociable to those you see when you're out and about. "See and be seen" is old show biz lore, but it makes good business sense, too. The reason being, a lot can be achieved with a simple run-in.

I'll give you a good example this time. Lori and I went to a party not long ago at Jimmy and Molly Kimmel's house. (They have their own pizza oven—how cool is that?!?) Louis CK was there, and the two of us BS'd for a while. I was bitching to Louis about how my agent at the time was great with writing gigs, but didn't have great contacts for my stand-up and corporate connections. Louis went on to sing the praises of his agent, who excelled in both areas. And then he said he would be happy to mention me to him. That led to me signing with his agent, who got me a book deal. So a casual conversation at a party turned into me selling this very book (to you).

I make a point of mentioning this detail because I know Louis only casually. He opened for me a couple of times when he was coming up and I was a headliner. Calling him about my agency predicament would've been nothing short of weird. We're not close enough for that kind of exchange. But at a party, it wasn't a strange conversation at all. And when things like that happen organically, through the course of simply talking at a party, it's pretty stellar.

There's no predicting which encounters will be the ones that take your career to a new and interesting place. So always be social. Get up and go across a room to say hi. Great things can result. Even if all you get out of it is a cool conversation, it's worth doing. As for the awkward, uncomfortable outcomes . . . well, they're valuable in a different way. This wouldn't have been much of a story if Harry Dean Stanton had immediately greeted me with, "Of course I remember you, Carol. How you doing, Mommy?"

Richard Belzer and Harry Dean, from my end of the dinner table at the Palm.

PART
TWO

HOW TO MAINTAIN YOUR SANITY

WHILE STUBBORNLY ADVANCING

AN EVER-ARDUOUS CAREER

"There's not just one thing, Carol."

—Jerry Seinfeld

# CHAPTER 9

## THE SINGER, THEN THE VENTRILOQUIST, THEN THE CHICK

The question I get asked the most—besides "What is Jerry Seinfeld really like?"—is "What's it like being a woman in a male-dominated business?" From day one of my journey till now, my response has always been the same. Being female is a tremendous advantage, and always will be.

People are surprised by that answer, especially women. Many want to hear me complain about how it's a tougher road, the opportunities are not equal, and so on. But instead of focusing on all the negatives, it's always been my philosophy to focus on the distinct benefits that being female brings to the workplace. Many times, women just don't open their eyes to see them. So take a good look around, ladies, because they're out there. And for you guys reading this, don't skip to the next chapter. Some of these advantages are things you can emulate, too (without losing your inherent "dudeness").

The initial benefit I encountered as an up-and-coming stand-up was that I got onstage a lot more often than my male counterparts. Purely because I was female. Only a handful of women were doing stand-up back when I started, and the owners of clubs would put together lineups in this manner: "Well, we'll start out with the singer, then the ventriloquist, then the woman comic, then the impressionist . . . ," and so on. As sexist as that was, putting not just a "comic" onstage, but a "woman comic," *I got on*. Which is a lot more than I can say about the warehouse full of white male comics who littered the bar, waiting to get a break. (Not much has changed over the years; even today, stand-up has all the diversity of the crowd at the X Games.)

As much as it didn't feel good being marginalized as a "specialty act" just because I had a pair of boobs, I still got my stage time. Which is what any comic wants and needs. You've got to be terrible before you get good. And believe me, when I started I had some sets that ended so badly you could have put police tape around them. But that's true in most careers—you have to be bad at it when you start (though not, hopefully, if your career is cardiac surgery). So the more I got on stage, the more I knew I was on my way to becoming a better comedian. If you're working in a mostly male environment, being a woman might get you noticed, as unfair as that may be. So be prepared to use that time in the spotlight to gain the skills and experience that will further your career.

Here's another advantage: women see the world differently than men do. (Maybe it's because when we look at the opposite sex, our eyes aren't focused six inches below the face.) We have unique experiences that are worlds away from those of a man. I exploited that quality in finding material for my act. Not in an "Am I right, ladies?" way (although I am right about this, ladies), but from the observational approach that everyone uses in creating a comedy routine.

For example, I talked onstage about how women would go on dates with guys, order a "dinner salad," and then go home and binge their face off. (Maybe not the most radical observation today, but thirty-five years ago, not many people were talking about this stuff.) It got big laughs because women, as well as men, knew how true it was. Maybe some couples in the audience that very night were about to experience this particular quirk together.

So club owners started to see that it was a good idea to put women comics in their lineups, because the audience would hear a perspective that hadn't been expressed in comedy very often, even though it was a perspective held by half the audience.

I also developed a good habit back in those days, one that I continue today—I steal from the tip jar. No, just kidding. The habit is this: I ask for help. And that's another advantage a woman brings to the workplace. Now, to be clear, I'm not positing this idea as a "poor me/I'm subservient" fallback to make up for a woman's supposed physical weakness. Quite the contrary. I'm suggesting it as a very powerful tool for professional success that you should have in your arsenal. Whatever the career path, at some point everyone needs feedback, advice, and occasional TLC to help them advance. And I do think women have been socialized to ask for help more easily than men. (When's the last time you heard a man under sixty ask for help opening a stuck window? Or with anything else, for that matter?)

Make no mistake: men can be especially helpful to women, because guys can help us understand men. That's key for any female who's in the minority at work. I can point to clear examples of how getting that kind of help created huge gains for me.

Here's one. As a comic, I always asked other comics to watch my act, to get a realistic gauge on my progress and lend an objective eye to stage problems I was trying to fix. Early in my career, I was having a hard time with groups of men in the audience. If three or more guys came in and sat together at a table, at some point during my set they would inevitably give me a hard time and heckle me. (At comedy clubs—like most everywhere else, I suppose—anytime more than two guys get together, they take on a packlike mentality. The difference being that pack animals don't wear too much Axe cologne.) I swear you could have set your watch to it, especially if the guys were on the younger side. I just never had the right comebacks or attitude onstage to make it stop.

So one night at the Improv I asked a fellow comic, whose act revolved a lot around guys and their way of thinking, if he would watch my set. (I had seen a bunch of bridge-and-tunnel guys waiting to come into the showroom, and I had a pretty good hunch they would hassle me that night. Which they did.) When my set was done, the comic came over, and after first kindly consoling me (sets like that, where guys pummeled me from the audience, were *brutal*, and comedians are a surprisingly fraternal bunch), he went on to pinpoint where I'd gone wrong in my attempts to shut them down. He told me, "They're guys out on a Saturday night, and there are no women with them—that's their Achilles heel. They don't want to be reminded of that, much less in front of the crowd. So there's your assault weapon right there."

Sure enough, the next time I went onstage and was heckled by the Young Guy Table, I responded with, "Hey, guys. Where's all your dates tonight? Still parking the car I guess, huh?" Like I'd waved a magic wand, anytime I used this line, the heckling usually stopped. (The one or two times the heckling did continue, I just had to add "Well, no wonder you're alone tonight," and that would end it for good.) It's a survival strategy I still use onstage to this day. It took a guy to show me that zeroing in on the stag status of these bozos would be enough to shut them up. I don't think I would have ever found the solution had it not been for the camaraderie of someone who knew what makes the male brain tick, because he had one of his own.

Another way that I believe I've made gains compared to my male colleagues, and how you might, too, is that I'm a good listener. I do think that quality was encouraged in me as part of my upbringing as a girl. As biased as that might have been, I've found it to be a tremendous asset, especially in the business I'm in. No one listens in the entertainment business, because they only want to talk about their next project, or in the case of comedians, they don't pay attention to what you're saying because they want to try out new material, even during normal conversation. ("Glad to hear you had a great vacation, Carol. And speaking of flying, have you ever noticed . . .") So annoying. I can't tell you how many lunches and meetings I've had where I've just been a sympathetic ear to a man who seemed to want to vent about anything and everything, especially his love life (they have no idea how many times I've secretly agreed with the wife). After the encounter, I've been in a good place with that person work-wise, and I always credit it to being an engaged audience for them. Who doesn't like to talk and be heard? (That's a founding principle for the organization Hadassah, by the way.)

So, to me, your attitude as a woman at work can always be distilled to a half-empty or half-full perspective. You can bitch and moan about being outnumbered, or you can find the scenarios in which being female is the biggest break you could ever hope for. Granted, not all the advantages I had will apply in your situation; you're probably not taking numbers to get a turn telling jokes at next Wednesday's sales meeting (though maybe you should; I hear the quarterlies aren't looking too good). But once you start thinking about it, I'm sure you can come up with some

XX-chromosome-related benefits of your own. Take the things that made you cringe about being raised a girl and spin them into your own Wonder Woman powers.

If your comedy club is named Tickles,
is it really necessary to include a feather?

# Carol Leifer

appearing on

## "Late Night with David Letterman"
Thursday, April 4th, 12:30 a.m.

and

## "The Merv Griffin Show"
Monday, April 15th, 9:00 p.m.

# CHAPTER 10

## DON'T DEVELOP A DRINKING PROBLEM

I don't have a drinking problem. But that doesn't mean there wasn't a time when I drank too much.

It started slowly, back in 1982. Paul Reiser and I were booked to do a gig at a college in Vermont. I was set to open the show, with Paul closing. We left New York City early, estimating an arrival time of six p.m., giving us plenty of time to relax before our eight o'clock show.

But with one wrong turn somewhere off US-7, we were screwed. This was a primitive time, before cell phones and GPS. We had to use *maps*. Which, as anyone over thirty knows, are just evil pieces of origami.

As a result, we didn't pull onto the campus until eight-fifteen or so. We scrambled to find the student union, made our apologies, and hustled backstage. (Which wasn't even a true "backstage," just a stairwell off the auditorium.)

As we waited to go on, Paul asked how long a set I was planning to do: "A half hour each? Does that sound about right, Leafless?" (His nickname for me.)

"I can't go on just yet, Paul," I answered. "I can't."

"Do you need a few minutes?"

"I need more than a few minutes. For sure."

I guess I said it with such stark desperation that Paul never even questioned me. The moment registered, and then he just calmly told me, "Okay, I'll go up first. Take whatever time you need, Leaf."

And as Paul stepped onstage to the waiting college crowd, I did what I needed to do: I pulled out the two mini-bottles of white wine that I had taken from a recent airline flight, unscrewed the twist-off tops, and downed both pretty quickly. As I sat there in that musty stairwell, I knew something had gone horribly wrong.

Drinking before going onstage had started innocently enough, about three years earlier. I'd gotten one of my first big breaks. A booker had come into the Comic Strip in New York City and auditioned acts for his West Coast club called the Laff Stop (are the names for comedy clubs epic or what?), which had locations in Claremont and Newport Beach, California. It was a big deal, and an honor, to be booked out there. I had done only local gigs up to that point. Flying out to California at twenty-two years old, all by myself, to perform in a comedy club that I wasn't familiar with turned my normal preperformance jitters into near paralysis.

So I got to California. And there I was with some time to kill before my first show, pacing nervously by the bar, when a friendly bartender asks, "How 'bout a drink?" I'd never had any alcohol before going onstage before—sure, maybe a glass of wine or two afterward. But this bartender was nice, and offering. And as I was, conveniently, scared as all hell, I figured why not.

Lo and behold, one glass of wine later and the first set of my California adventure was a smash. I was loose and in the moment. All my anxiety melted away, and I was having big-time fun onstage.

Stand-up comedy is a monster. Performing it is like walking a tightrope with no net. Or at least, not a very big one. When you're killing, you feel like Leonardo DiCaprio standing on the bow of the ship in *Titanic*. And when you're bombing . . . well, you feel like you're on the actual *Titanic*. You'll never feel as small in your life as you do when your set is going badly. You literally count the seconds until you can get offstage and disappear far, far away. And here was this easy fix: drinking. It removed all the risk and bad stuff. It was a magic way to make everything exactly the way it should be.

Until that moment in the stairwell . . .

The thing I was naive enough not to know was that the one glass of wine that first got me buzzed and feeling good during a performance soon became two glasses. And though at the beginning I would just grab a glass here or there before going onstage, before long I had to be sure to get to a club a good half hour or so before I went on, so I could time my buzz *just right*. This elixir was proving tricky to manage.

It all came crashing down in Vermont as I pounded down that wine, listening to the laughs that Paul was already getting out on stage. This little shortcut I'd thought I'd found was making things mighty complicated. Thanks, United Airlines! Maybe if your peanuts hadn't been so heavily salted, I wouldn't have been so thirsty before that first California set, and I could have avoided this mess to begin with.

So, right then and there, I decided to stop drinking. Just like that, cold turkey. (Which, of course, sounds like a drink itself or, at the very least, Wild Turkey's emotionally detached brother.)

This decision turned out to be quite fortuitous, because two weeks later I got my first booking on *Late Night with David Letterman*. I was to appear on the show in three months. Getting smashed before my network television debut, in an NBC green room with bottles of bad airline wine piled everywhere, was *not* going to be part of the plan.

At first, it was hard to do stand-up without getting snockered. I basically had to relearn how to perform, removing alcohol from the equation. I needed to take all that raw nervousness and anxiety and use it to fuel my act. It took a few months, but when I finally internalized this concept, it was quite a revelation. I learned that the nerves and fear *never* leave a stand-up comic (except for Jay Leno, who is hands-down the most relaxed comedian I've ever known). It's a part of the game that, for some foolish reason, I thought would go away with time. But it doesn't. And as a comic, when you can learn how to harness the engine of that fear, it makes your performance that much better.

Performing is a particularly nerve-wracking way to make a living. But any career comes with its risky, high-pressure moments, and there's no quick-fix substitute for learning to ride that fear. When you succeed in doing that, you also learn another invaluable lesson: how not to look nervous even though you are. I'm really proud of my twenty-six stand-up appearances on *Late Night with David Letterman*. But I was nervous each and every time. If you watch a clip of any of them, you'll see that after my set, as I walked to the desk to talk with Dave, he whispered something in my ear:

"Carol, your hands are ICE COLD!" he'd say, slightly shocked. And I'd giggle with embarrassment.

Since that night in Vermont, I've never taken another drink before going onstage. And I'm happy to report that this unhappy dance with the hooch didn't spill over into other parts of my life. Thank the good Lord, because Mommy does love her cocktails!

But the best part of this story is that, to this day, Paul Reiser has never asked me what the hell was up that night. I needed a friend in the worst way in that moment, and Paul came through with flying colors. Simple as that. It's one of the things I'm most grateful for in my career.

There's a bond among the comedians I started out with, my "class," that's as strong as a chain link. I don't doubt that

Eddie Murphy or Rosie O'Donnell would have done the exact same thing for me that night. Comics get each other in a way that nobody else does because we do the same nutty work. And as much as I have a wonderful family and a partner and old friends I've known since grade school, no one will ever understand a comedian like another comedian.

So, don't develop a drinking problem. Or a drug problem, or an M&M problem, or any problem that arises from trying to cheat your way around the stresses and fears that come with your chosen profession. Always be wary of the easy way out. I had this poster hung up on my wall in college, and damn if it isn't as true today as it was back then: "The best way out is always through." (At the very least, it's holding up much better than my Loggins and Messina poster.)

With Paul Reiser backstage in Atlantic City, 1982.

# CHAPTER 11

## WHO ELSE IS A PROCTOLOGIST GONNA TALK TO?

Back when I was starting out in New York, I got booked to do a corporate gig, and like most of these jobs, it was in a hotel ballroom. Typically, my agent would book these gigs, but I would go by myself. I've always been pretty low maintenance and don't require much hand holding.

So I arrived at the job to find two of the three things that a comedian requires to do a show: a microphone and a stand to hold it. But not the third: a spotlight.

"Excuse me," I said as I approached the tech guy. "Who is going to be working the follow spot for me tonight?"

"I'm not sure what you're talking about," he replied.

"It was in the contract," I tried to remind him. "It's the spotlight to follow me while I perform."

The dude looked at me blankly and then said, "Well, we don't have it." Only he said it as if he was annoyed, like, "Oh, get a load of this diva. We don't have *her spotlight!*" As if I was Cher or something.

So, while making a mental note that my agent needed to double check this detail for future gigs—like a lot of things in my haphazard profession—I decided to grin and bear it.

That is, until a fellow comic stepped in and came to the rescue . . .

I was fortunate enough to be introduced by Joan Rivers, who'd been booked for a brief appearance at the event. Sure enough, Joan strode into that ballroom (agent-less, as I was), and like any pro she got an immediate lay of the land. It didn't take one minute.

"Where's her spotlight?" Joan asked.

"Huh?" Mr. I-Could-Give-a-Crap responded.

"Carol's follow spot. Where is it?"

"Ummm . . . ," the tech mumbled. Then, pointing to me, he said, "I told her I don't know."

"Well, that's just unacceptable," Joan said. "That's an important element of her show. It brings a sense of focus to the audience."

The dude just shrugged helplessly as a frustrated Joan bounded onstage. After a couple minutes of doing her thing, Joan turned to my introduction.

"Look, I'm just a pop-in guest here," Joan said to the crowd. "But the woman who's going to entertain you for the bulk of the evening has a big stumbling block ahead. You shtummies didn't provide a spotlight for her. And lest you think that's a trivial omission, it's not. You'd know that if you were me, but you're car salesmen! So give her your full attention, because I'll accept nothing less!"

My hero.

After giving the tech guy a solid "toldja so!" look, I walked onstage. And lemme tell ya, that audience gave me everything and more. (Would you want to face the wrath of Joan Rivers?!)

All it took to turn things around was another comic to fully understand my situation. And here's the lesson behind this particular incident: Make sure you *cultivate a fellowship with the people you work with*, because that will come in handy in times like these.

Whatever you do for a living, no one will ever understand your job like someone who does it, too. My partner, Lori, is my rock and foundation. We've been together for seventeen years, and I don't know where I'd be without her daily love and support. Yet, when I have work-related concerns or problems, as much as I love my Lori, I usually turn to fellow writers or comics for advice. Lori doesn't take it personally. As with me, when she has challenges in her work—real estate—she knows that I'm not an expert (although I have heard it bandied about that location is important). So, on your professional journey, I encourage you to forge strong bonds with your peers. You've got to watch out for one another, because sometimes a fellow member of the club is the only one who gets it.

This is one of the reasons very little joke-stealing happens in the world of stand-up. Oh believe me, people try, and some may get away with it. But word gets around quickly. And in comedy, as soon as a thief is discovered . . . Well, it's not exactly the mob. The offender won't be shot and buried in a landfill somewhere in New Jersey. But that may be the only venue he ends up playing.

Here's another reason to cultivate professional camaraderie. In any work situation, you have to protect your reputation, especially among peers. If you're hitting it out of the park with your clients but are not particularly well liked by your coworkers, you're setting yourself up for a big fall. Because someday you'll need the support of your brethren, and they'll be more than happy to step out of the way as you stumble. I've seen it happen a thousand times.

So, love what you do. But also see the value in connecting with the other people who do what you do. It's a principle that probably applies to any vocation out there. When I think about a job like, say, proctology . . . medical degree aside, that seems like the most unsavory job anyone could have. Yet I'm sure that when all those colorectal surgeons get together at their annual Proctologist's Convention, what a hoot this bunch must have comparing notes on patients. Oh man, the stories (that I'd love to miss). As I'm sure they'd all agree, no two assholes are alike—certainly in their business, and in whatever endeavor you choose, too.

**The Federated Group**

YOUR STEREO·VIDEO SUPERSTORES

5655 East Union Pacific Avenue
City of Commerce, California 90022
(213) 728-5100

Dear Mr. Jeff Patterson,

    It is my understanding that you are the agent for Carol
Leifer and Larry Miller.  On the night of thursday, August 27,
both Mr. Miller and Miss Leifer were doing a show at the L.A.
Marriot for The Federated Group's annual EXPO.  My name is ▮▮▮▮
▮▮▮▮ and I would like to apologize for any actions or comments
I may have made to the entertainers.  I was way out of line and
I truly am sorry. Thank you for having such talented and professional entertainers.  I hope my actions didn't discourage
them from doing shows of this kind in the future.

                          Sincerely,

This is an apology letter I received after a horrible corporate gig.
I wish more bosses made their drunk employees send these!

# CHAPTER 12

## HECKLED BY STEPHEN HAWKING

There was a point in my career as a road comic that I unaffectionately refer to as the "comedy condo" years. Basically, club owners got smart. Their epiphany was: "Why should I pay to put up my comedians in a reputable midpriced hotel when I can simply buy a cheap condo and toss them all in there for the week?" Of course, what the club owners didn't consider were all the amenities that hotels provide for their guests. Simple things, like daily maid service and a secure environment. But as much as I hated these condos, they were, unfortunately, a deal breaker with my gig offers. Anytime my agent requested a hotel for me instead, the answer was always a resounding "take it or leave it."

Occasionally, these comedy condo gigs had a silver lining: I got to work with a friend. So I was very happy when my agent scored me a week-long gig in Phoenix with my buddy and fellow comic Sue Kolinsky. Comedy condo or not, nothing beats having a pal along to brave the uncertainties of a week in a strange town.

Fresh from the airport, Sue and I arrived at the comedy

condo and were greeted by the usual suspect, a friendly thirtyish white guy, the probable opening act (Sue was middling and I was the headliner). He showed us the other two rooms available, and Sue and I planted roots with our suitcases. Looking around, I saw that this comedy condo was pretty standard—not the cleanest ever (the kitchens in these places, oddly, never seemed to have a single sponge). But there was a swimming pool, so that raised its score by many points. Sue and I put on our bathing suits and enjoyed a couple of hours by the pool with White Guy before having to head over to the club.

Around seven p.m., now freshly showered and dressed, Sue and I went to the front door to head out to the venue. As was typical, we waited for White Guy so we could all go together. But he was nowhere to be found. Sue shouted, "We're ready to go down to the club! You coming?" The next thing we knew, White Guy, still dressed in his swim trunks, came to the front door to tell us, "No, thanks. I don't need a ride."

"Well, how are you going to get over to the club?" I asked him.

"And you're still not dressed," Sue commented.

"Oh, I'm not a comic," he said blankly. "I just live here."

Seems the slimy club owners also learned that renting out rooms to complete strangers made the condo an even smarter investment decision. Sometimes I wonder how this story never wound up on NBC's *Dateline*.

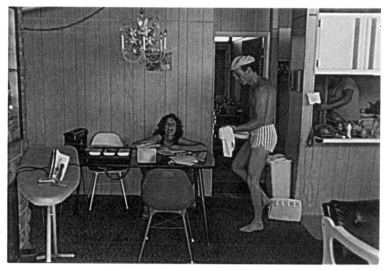

At the comedy condo. Which of these people is not a comedian?

Trust me, one day you'll have your own work horror stories to share (if you don't already). These things are just part of everyone's journey pursuing a career. I hope that knowing this fact ahead of time will help you have a sense of humor when a workplace disaster inevitably lands on your head.

When I started to earn real money doing stand-up, it was such a thrill. Going from making cab fare (five bucks) to an actual paying gig—the feeling was phenomenal. These first bookings were mostly what we called "Jersey gigs," clubs in New Jersey towns, like Long Branch, Asbury Park, and West Orange, that were all clamoring to be part of the comedy boom. Mind you, I use the word "club" loosely. Five minutes before, these "clubs" had been Knights of Columbus meeting halls, or the occasional sub place that lost its license because of food code violations. Jersey gigs paid around forty bucks, which might not seem like a lot now, but I can't even begin to describe the feeling of cold hard cash in your pocket earned simply from telling jokes.

One night, it was the usual drill. I was set to meet the driver in front of the Improv at Forty-fourth and Ninth who'd take me out to one of these Jersey towns. This guy pulls up in a beat-up '72 Duster. When I get in, I notice that the car has no rearview mirror. I became slightly alarmed, and I pointed it out to my driver. (I also use the word "driver" loosely. Five minutes ago, the "driver" was probably stealing this car.)

The guy says to me, "Don't worry, honey. I get the entire picture from the sides." Meaning, I assumed, the side mirrors. "Most people are not aware that the rearview is purely optional." Maybe he considered brakes as just a suggestion, too.

It wasn't just getting to and from the clubs that provided moments I'd rather forget. I've made some big mistakes onstage over the years that still make me shudder. I once worked at a dive in Pittsburgh where I was being heckled mercilessly. I mean, the guy just wouldn't let up. And to make matters worse, he was doing it in this odd, breathy voice. This was around the time that *Return of the Jedi* came out, and I figured he was doing a parody of Darth Vader. So I started to go at him good.

"Oh, big man doing his big *Star Wars* impression with the funny voice! Why don't you get up here on stage and then see how it goes?"

The guys heckles back, "I can't go up on stage."

"Well, of course," I said, "because you're a coward, asshole."

"No," he said. "I can't go up on stage because I'm *crippled*, that's why."

I put my hand over my eyes to shield the stage lights, and I looked out into the audience to find that the heckler was, in fact, a guy in a wheelchair. Not exactly the kind of "rolling in the aisles" that a comedian dreams of. And he was using an electronic voice box because he didn't have a larynx. *Oh, perfect. I thought. I'm being heckled by Stephen Hawking.*

I'm still not exactly sure what the expression "being run out of town on a rail" means, but I've always thought that if ever there was an opportunity for that to happen to me, it would have been that night. I literally had to be escorted to the car, so anxious was that crowd to tar and feather me. (That expression I can pretty much figure out.)

So, never forget these words: "This, too, shall pass." Console yourself during the difficult times with the thought that, if nothing else, you're banking some great stories to tell down the road. And please, if you ever come to one of my shows—disabled, fully abled, somewhere in between—don't heckle me. I swear, I still get spooked every time I see a handicap parking space.

# CHAPTER 13

## *SNL*: HIRED BY A U.S. SENATOR, DONE IN BY POLITICS

*Saturday Night Live* premiered in 1975, while I was in college, and comedy would never be the same. From the minute the show went on the air, it popped right off the screen as fresh and funny, and it immediately set a new standard for television comedy that continues today. So, in 1985 I was excited as anything when *SNL*'s creator, Lorne Michaels, returned to the helm after Dick Ebersol's five-year reign. And even more excited to hear that the show was setting up auditions for new cast members at the Comic Strip, my home-base comedy club in New York City.

The night of the audition, I saw Al Franken walk into the club. Yes, that's now Senator Al Franken. (And if you're too young to find that disconcerting, imagine this in twenty years: Vice President Daniel Tosh.) I was familiar with Al from his appearances on the show with his comedy partner, Tom Davis, and was a huge fan. A fellow comic mentioned that he'd heard Al was going to be an occasional performer and producer on the show that year. He also mentioned that the head writer, Jim

Downey, was part of the *SNL* posse that came to see the auditions. I had no idea if these things were true. When it comes to gossip, my fellow comics could put a couple of Boca yentas to shame. But I was excited nevertheless.

When you audition at a comedy club, it's risky, because you're at the mercy of two mercurial variables: the crowd and the performance order. You never know what audience is going to show up. They might be friendly and supportive. Or they might be drunk and hostile (a.k.a. every comedy club audience in Trenton, New Jersey). On the one hand, if you go on stage too early in the lineup, the crowd may not be warmed up enough to respond well. On the other hand, when you go on too late, your audience is leaning toward "tired" and/or "one cocktail too many."

It turns out I had some good karma the night of my *SNL* audition. I went on near the early middle of the lineup, a great spot. And as luck would have it, a warm and receptive audience showed up that night. (Little did those two hundred people know they were going to have a big say in the comedic fates of a dozen comedians.) I did better than I'd hoped.

After my set, I hung out at the bar, relieved and happy it had gone well. A few other comics had stand-out sets that night, too. Then, as the *Saturday Night Live* crew was leaving the club, Al Franken and Jim Downey came over to me, telling me that they thought I was funny and did a great job. They said I'd hear from them soon.

"You'll hear from us soon" is to show business what "I'll call you" is to one-night stands. But a week later my agent got a call: they liked my audition and now wanted me to meet Lorne Michaels. I was ecstatic! I was gonna meet Lorne over at a rehearsal studio on the West Side of Manhattan. I walked into the room, said hello, and shook hands with him. He told me that Al Franken and Jim Downey had highly recommended me to be a writer on the show, and I said I was glad to hear it. Then Lorne asked, "You know the hours are crazy on this show, don't you? Oftentimes, writers sleep in their offices the night before the read-throughs. Are you okay with that?" I emphatically assured him that I was, even though I wasn't exactly certain what a "read-through" was. And that was it. The meeting lasted maybe two minutes. I wasn't sure if that was good or not, until the next day when they called my agent and said that SNL did indeed want to hire me as a writer. I'll admit I was disappointed not to be offered a spot as a cast member, but I was also thrilled as hell to be offered any kind of job from this comedic institution. (The job also couldn't have come at a better time. I was recently separated from my husband, a fellow comic, and the SNL hire got me out of Los Angeles and back to New York. The distance away from my impending divorce helped enormously.)

I found an apartment in New York within walking distance to the show. To this day, I've had few experiences that rivaled working in Manhattan at legendary 30 Rock, and simply putting on a pair of sneakers to get there. The job got me into the union, the Writers Guild, and I was making their minimum, fifteen hundred dollars a week, which was a fortune to me at the time.

I'll call the season that I worked on *SNL* the "weird cast" one. Totally out-of-the-box hires like Joan Cusack, Randy Quaid, Robert Downey Jr., Jon Lovitz. The only comedians hired whom I knew were A. Whitney Brown and Dennis Miller. (Whitney was hired as a supporting player, and Dennis was a full-time player).

Once I started writing for the show, a clear pattern emerged. I had been hired by Al Franken and Jim Downey, not Lorne Michaels. Which was strange; it felt like being asked to play on a Beatles album by Ringo. No disrespect at all to Al and Jim. They're great guys with great comic minds. But it was clear that there was one leader at *SNL*. Period.

So, from day one I was never really part of Lorne Michael's "group." He had clear favorites among the performers and writers, the ones whom he invited to dinner and events. Subtlety was never Lorne's forte. You'd walk out of a meeting with him and twenty other people, and Lorne pretty much singled out those he wanted to join him to eat afterward. I always felt left out because, well, I was.

And not just socially. Lorne never really responded to many of my pitches, and when I handed in my sketches I didn't get much feedback from him. But I wasn't too concerned, since Franken and Downey remained huge supporters. They approved a lot of my pitches, so much so that Al and I wound up writing a few sketches together. And they were both very complimentary of the sketches that I did get on the air (although there weren't a ton of them).

What made matters worse was that the more I felt Lorne rebuke me, the more I pulled away. I'd even purposely avoid him if I saw him coming down the hall or chatting with people. I felt the best way to handle his indifference toward me was to just stay out of his way.

Lorne Michaels has a small sign on his desk at *SNL*, and it reads "The Captain's Word Is Law." It's a fitting nautical reference, since at times working there felt like being caught in a perfect storm. (From what I hear, it still graces his desk twenty-eight years later.) I really should have gotten the clear message from that sign. Instead of running away, I should have tried to penetrate his inner circle and draw out of him more thoughts on my work and how to make an impact at the show. Basically, I should not have taken his "no" for an answer. Plain and simple, pleasing Al and Jim didn't mean I was pleasing Lorne. I should have been more aware of that, instead of foolishly thinking I was somehow protected by being liked by his Number Twos.

I wound up getting fired at the end of the season. (Well, not really "fired." It's a weird system there. They simply never call your agent and ask you back.) But no hard feelings. I wasn't fully ready to become a writer then, and I did long to get back to my stand-up full-time. That turned out to be the right decision, because my act really grew and flourished most after my writing job at *SNL*. After all, I'd been part of an all-star team of writers that included Jack Handey, Don Novello, John Swartzlander, George Meyer, Bruce McCulloch, Mark McKinney, and Robert Smigel, who was an "apprentice" writer at the time (I used to tease him that it was a guild regulation that he always wear safety goggles while writing sketches).

Still, I wish I knew then what I know now, and I hope you'll benefit from knowing now what I didn't know then. Whatever workplace you're in, *always* aim to please the captain. It matters, even if the first mate is ecstatic with your performance, because it's the captain who ultimately decides who stays onboard. If, like I did, you sense that the one person in charge isn't thrilled with what you're doing, ask for feedback and figure out how to correct your course. Because flying under the radar is a passive tactic that will eventually get you tossed off the ship.

Can you pick out the only woman on the *SNL* writing staff?
Top row: Don Novello, John Swartzwelder, Mark McKinney, Jack Handey, Tom Davis.
Middle row: Bruce McCulloch, Robert Smigel, Carol Leifer, George Meyer.
Bottom row: A. Whitney Brown, Lanier Laney, Terry Sweeney, Lorne Michaels,
Al Franken, James Downey.

# CHAPTER 14

## FRANK SINATRA CALLED ME BIG

Don't think that the deepest valley of your career can't produce the greatest moment of your life.

If there's one constant I've experienced through all my many years in business, it's that there are peaks and valleys. (Another constant? Somebody always shoves a bottle of water in my hand before going in for a TV pitch. It's a meeting, people, not a 5K race.) Whatever your calling, the real test of your career longevity will come during the valleys. How will you rally and pick yourself up during those downtimes? That's the true challenge.

In 1989, I was deep in the valley.

My stand-up bookings were going from bad to worse. My agency couldn't even get me arrested. (This was back when an arrest didn't get you the cover of *People* and a series deal.) It can happen with talent agencies. They pay lots of attention to you in the "honeymoon phase," but after a while they start to lose interest and think there's someone newer, younger, and better out there. Sort of what it must be like to date George Clooney.

So, I was pleasantly surprised when I went on vacation in

St. Thomas and ran into Rodney Dangerfield's agent . . . let's call him Shecky. I'd met him a year earlier when Rodney had picked me to be part of his HBO Young Comedians special. Shecky asked how my career was going, and I shared how disappointed I was that I didn't get a bigger pop from the Rodney special. Shecky suggested I get in touch when we were both back in New York. He said he'd love to sit down and talk about representing me. I was over the moon.

Three weeks later, I met with Shecky at his office in Midtown Manhattan. We reviewed the gigs I had done over the past year, where they were, and how much I was paid. Shecky was not impressed, to put it mildly.

"You did Governor's Comedy Club on Long Island for fourteen hundred dollars? Man, they got you cheap."

"Coconuts only paid you two grand? They sure hit bargain basement when they booked you!"

And on and on . . . Shecky scoffed at every single gig I'd done over the last twelve months. Then he assured me that if I signed with him, he would raise my price dramatically and I would easily be earning twice what I had been. Making that decision seemed like an absolute no-brainer.

Cut to six months later . . .

Not only was I not earning double what I made before, but the gigs Shecky did land me were the bottom of the barrel. Like . . . a stand-up gig at the Ground Round restaurant on the

Jersey Turnpike. For those of you unfamiliar with the franchise, it's like Applebee's, minus the pretension. One of the charms of the chain was that diners threw their discarded peanut shells on the restaurant's sawdust floor. Imagine trying to land jokes against the background of that nutty din.

I just didn't get it. I would call Shecky regularly and ask him what was up. Where were all the plum dates with the big ka-ching? "Carol, I'm working on a big gig for you. Opening for Frank, so sit tight."

Dinner at the captain's table, a perk of working a cruise.
But . . . who's steering the ship?

"Frank, who?" I would ask incredulously. "Frank Stallone? Because that's around the level of the gigs you've been getting me."

"Frank Sinatra," Shecky said. "In *Vegas*."

Oh, sure. You can't get me beyond a Jersey Turnpike exit. Opening for Frank Sinatra? Yeah, like that's gonna happen.

I scraped along as best I could the next few months. I took any gig Shecky threw me, because what else could I do? And each time I would call and confront him about my situation, it was an exact replay of the conversation we'd had countless time before.

"Frank, Carol. Frank!"

About six months later, I was working a cruise ship to Bermuda. (A gig, I might add, that I booked myself. I had given up on Shecky and started to solicit myself to anyone who had a legitimate gig, on land or at sea.) One day while I was playing paddle tennis on the upper deck, an announcement came over the loud speaker:

"CAROL LEIFER! CAROL LEIFER! PHONE CALL FOR CAROL LEIFER!"

My heart raced. In 1989, if you got a telephone call on a cruise ship, it meant one of two things. Either your house had burned down or a parent had died.

But in my case there was a third option. It was Shecky, calling to say that he had just booked me to open for Frank Sinatra. I was shocked! So much so that I made only one trip that night to the midnight buffet.

And lo and behold, a month later I opened for Frank Sinatra at Bally's hotel in Las Vegas. Turned out, Shecky knew Sinatra's manager Jilly Rizzo very well, and that led to my booking. It was as surreal an experience as I'll ever have. I met Mr. Sinatra before the first show. Jilly escorted me to his dressing room. And I met Frank Sinatra—while he was wearing the top half of his tux and only boxer shorts on the bottom. Still, even half-dressed . . . *I'm meeting Frank Sinatra!*

I did four shows with Mr. Sinatra, and they all went like gangbusters. To a large degree I attribute that success to a piece of advice my good friend and fellow comic Larry Miller shared with me. I told Larry before the gig that I was really nervous. As rabid as Sinatra's fans were, why would they want to endure the girl comic beforehand?

Larry said, "Carol, you've got it all wrong. The audience is going to be looking at you like, 'This is Frank's girl! He chose her out of everyone to be his opening act, so she must be fantastic.'"

Larry was right on the money. I opened each show with, "I was so happy when Mr. Sinatra asked me to join him here at Bally's . . ." And then I was off and running.

Frank Sinatra was a complete gentleman at all the shows I opened for him. First of all, he put my name on the marquee alongside his. I know that may not sound like much, but many of the stars in Vegas at that time wouldn't give their opening comics any billing. (My good friend Bill Maher once opened for a big star who wouldn't put his name up with hers. I won't say who, but her talent is *supreme*.) Second, at each and every show, Mr. Sinatra brought me back out for a bow before he started his set. What a class, class act.

**About to meet Mr. S.**

A couple of times, Mr. Sinatra even personally complimented me to the audience as I took my bow. At one show, he brought me back onstage and said, "That's one funny broad! I wish my mother had been that funny, I wouldn't have had to work so hard." On another night he said, "Carol Leifer! She's big! She'll knock you over for the phone!" To this day, I still wish I knew what he meant by that.

(As a writer, here's something I especially appreciate about Frank Sinatra: Before every song he performed, he would credit the composer and lyricist. He felt their artistry was so important that it merited mention. Frank was a breed of performer that's hard to find these days.)

Opening for Frank Sinatra remains the single greatest moment of my career. It's that rare thing when fantasy meets reality to such a surreal degree. And it happened at one of the lowest points of my career. Somehow, the stars were aligned the day I got that call on the cruise ship. (By the way, if you thought you don't like people on *land* . . .)

Unfortunately, that gig from Shecky was a fluke. Shecky and I stopped working together because, right after Frank, it was back to being booked at the "Ha Ha's" and "Sir Laff-a-Lots" of the comedy world.

But much like an idiot savant, Shecky will always be fondly remembered by me as my "agent savant." The dude got me gigs in some of the worst dives I've ever imagined, but he obliterated all of them in one fell swoop with that top-of-the-food-chain booking in Vegas.

So, when you find yourself in a career nadir of your own, take heart. Find humor in the situation if you can (see Chapter 12, "Heckled by Stephen Hawking"). Work hard to climb out of the valley. And keep in mind that once in a while, a deep dark crevasse may hide the most fantastic experience of your life.

And here's a suggestion to the Ground Round restaurants that still dot our nation's turnpikes: Edamame is a healthy low-sodium treat, and the shells are soft and quiet.

**ENTERTAINMENT INC.**

CONTRACT #1079

Agreement made this _____9th_____ day of _____June_____ 19 __89__

between _____ONE FELL SWOOP INC. f/s/o CAROL LEIFER_____

(hereinafter referred to as "ARTIST")

and _____BALLY'S HOTEL AND CASINO_____

(hereinafter referred to as "PURCHASER").

It is mutually agreed between the parties as follows:

The PURCHASER hereby engages the ARTIST and the ARTIST hereby agrees to perform the engagement hereinafter provided, upon all of the terms and conditions herein set forth, including those hereof entitled "Additional Terms and Conditions"

1. Date(s) of Engagement: Thursday, June 22 through Sunday, June 25, 1989
   total of 5 shows

2. Place of Engagement: Bally's Hotel and Casino
   3645 Las Vegas Blvd. South
   Exact Address: Las Vegas, NV 89109

3. Hours of Engagement: Thursday and Friday 6/22 and 23 at 9:00pm; Saturday 6/24 at 8:00 and 11:30pm; Sunday 6/25 at 8:30pm

4. Full Price Agreed Upon: $5,000 flat guarantee
   Artist to perform immediately preceeding Frank Sinatra

   BALLY'S COMPANY CHECK

   All payments shall be paid by ~~certified check, money order, bank draft or cash~~ as follows:
   (a) $ ___not applicable___ shall be paid by PURCHASER to and in the name of ARTIST'S agent, QBQ ENTERTAINMENT INC., not later than _____

   (b) $ ___$5,000.00___ shall be paid by PURCHASER to ARTIST not later than ___prior to performance___ on final night of engagement. Check payable to ONE FELL SWOOP INC.

   (c) Additional payments if any, shall be paid by PURCHASER to ARTIST not later than ___not applicable___.

PURCHASER shall first apply any and all receipts derived from the engagement herein to the payments required hereunder
   All payments shall be made in full without any deductions whatsoever

5. Scale of Admission: $50.00 per ticket minimum

   Return all signed copies to agent: _____ (ARTIST)
   QBQ ENTERTAINMENT INC.
   48 EAST 50th STREET        By ___ONE FELL SWOOP INC. f/s/o CAROL LEIFER___
   NEW YORK, N.Y 10022

   _____ (PURCHASER)

   By ___RICHARD STURM   for BALLY'S HOTEL AND CASINO___

   Address: 3645 Las VegasBlvd South

   Las Vegas, NV 89109

   Phone: 702-739-4611

The above signatures confirm that the parties have read and approve each and all of the "Additional Terms and Conditions" set forth on the reverse side hereof.
                    SEE REVERSE SIDE***

My "Frank" contract for Vegas.

# CHAPTER 15

## THE SHOW ABOUT NOTHING
## TAUGHT ME SOMETHING

Being a writer on *Seinfeld* was all about one thing—the big idea. That was the currency that kept you afloat or got you tossed.

And don't all businesses run on good ideas? Even if you're just selling hot dogs, you need to come up with ways to make people want your hot dogs more than the other guy's hot dogs (like, sell them with papaya juice). Sure, in some workplaces you can get pretty far by clocking in on time, complimenting the boss's tie, and never using more than your allotment of paper clips. But whatever your profession, I bet that sooner or later, a good idea will be the thing that gets you noticed.

At *Seinfeld*, we learned the importance of ideas pretty quickly. As soon as each season began, the first order of business was to secure time with Larry David and Jerry Seinfeld to go into their office and pitch. (Yes, *their* office. They were a team who worked with their desks literally pushed up against each other, like two concert pianists.)

Until you had a good idea that Larry and Jerry both loved

and signed off on, you didn't have squat to write. There were no "assignments" at *Seinfeld*. It was the only sitcom I've ever worked on that didn't have a "room"—that is, a group of writers sitting around a table littered with junk food, trying to come up with story ideas or "beat" (top) one another's jokes. In most places, the writers are assigned a script, and they go off and complete a first draft on their own. But when that first draft comes back, the bulk of the rewriting goes on in the "room."

Jerry and Larry in their office at *Seinfeld*.

Seinfeld was clearly its own animal, which is a big reason I was lucky enough to be hired in the first place. Larry and Jerry specifically wanted to hire writers who had never written on a network sitcom. So the mountain of spec scripts that had been submitted by seasoned writers from *Murphy Brown, Cheers,* and the other hit shows of the time were all nixed. The guys wanted a fresh perspective, from writers who came clean to the task. And being stand-up comics themselves, Larry and Jerry had a bent for hiring fellow stand-ups and buddies.

Pitching your ideas at *Seinfeld* was tough. Especially getting Larry David to bite. Larry had this physical tic when he was bored: he'd stretch his shoulder down from his neck and then move his arm around in a circle, looking like he was in pain. I'd pitch, Larry would listen while doing a lap with his shoulder, then at the end he'd often just shake his head and declare, "No, I don't love that one." I remember that the biggest putdown Larry could say after a pitch was "I could see that on another show." Ouch! Knowing the visceral disdain he had for sitcoms on network television, that piece of rejection always cut me to the bone.

But when a pitch worked, there was no better feeling. From the first day, I could tell that the number one rule of pitching to Larry and Jerry was to be concise. One or two sentences, which would hopefully be punctuated at the end by a big laugh from both of them. With anything too long, you could feel them drifting off and almost hear them thinking, "Get to it, man!"

Knowing that, I got straight to the point when I pitched "George brings a deaf woman to a party so she can lip-read his ex-girlfriend's lips to find out why she broke up with him." It broke Larry's shoulder spell. I knew I'd landed a winner because when he liked an idea, Larry would literally leap out of his chair and shout, "Yes! That's a show! We're doing that!"

(The inspiration for that episode came from listening to *The Howard Stern Show*. Kathy Buckley, a deaf comedian, had talked with Howard about what a proficient lip reader she was. It made me think that, were she a friend of mine, how I would have mined that superhero skill for personal gain!)

Pitching at Seinfeld also drove home a valuable strategy I'd learned as a stand-up comedian: to mine my own life—especially my life as a female (see Chapter 9, "The Singer, Then the Ventriloquist, Then the Chick")—for ideas that were distinctive and would set me apart. For example, it's doubtful that a male writer would have pitched "Elaine thinks the manicurists at her nail salon are talking about her in Korean behind her back." I'll never know for sure, but I still think the ladies were doing that at my nail place. (Though who cares; I get free manicures to this day because the owner's still thrilled that we used the real name of her store on the show.) Or "Elaine thinks that the mirrors at Barneys are skinny mirrors." I knew this one was a unique pitch for sure when I had to explain to the guys on staff what "skinny mirrors" are.

I was a fake date for a gay male friend once, accompanying him on an evening with his banker boss and wife at the Hollywood Bowl, which became the inspiration for the episode "The Beard." I can pretty much assure you that not one of the guys on staff had ever been a beard for a lesbian. And though I never dated a saxophone player, my imagination ran wild about what sexual act, if performed on a woman for too long, would ruin his embouchure—a story point of "The Marble Rye." (I still can't believe that in 1995 the network never gave us one bit of resistance to that episode. The perks of being on a hit show—they leave you alone!)

The only pitfall of being on the writing staff of TV's

On set with Jason Alexander.

Hello, Newman!

number one comedy was the constant flux of people coming up to you on a daily basis to share their brilliant ideas for the next episode. (Although the same thing would routinely happen to me as a comedian. People will tell you the worst or most offensive joke possible, or an incredibly boring anecdote, and then say, "You should put that in your act." Umm . . . no thanks.)

I usually took those *Seinfeld* suggestions with a polite grain of salt and then tried to move on as gracefully as I could. But when a friend from high school told me how this couple had gone to a dinner party, bringing a bread that was never served, and then they wound up taking the bread back home out of spite . . . I knew right away this was an idea that would make Larry leap to his feet. That idea morphed into the core story of the abovementioned classic "Marble Rye" episode. So whatever business you're in, always keep a friendly ear out for a random pitch that you can spin into something viable. As my mother (and many other Jewish women) used to say, "You never know . . . "

Side note: As a souvenir from that episode, I got to keep the empty industrial-size can of Beef-a-Reeno (Chef Boyardee wouldn't grant us permission to use the name Beef-a-Roni) that Kramer's horse Rusty devoured. I have few regrets in life, but one is that when I relocated, the moving men thought it was just an empty can and tossed it. Arghhhh!!!!!

Working at a show that had no writers' room turned out to be the best experience a new sitcom writer like me could ever have.

Most people are unaware that every episode of *Seinfeld* you see on the air was rewritten by Larry and Jerry. They had the final pass on each and every writer's draft, and when they were done, the script always turned out better and more finely tuned than what the writer originally handed in. To me, this was an opportunity: I pored over their drafts, studying which parts of my script they kept, what they threw out, and what they altered. I learned an invaluable amount. Whenever your ideas don't rise to the top, or if they get changed along the way, it's important to understand why.

I'll probably never have another writing experience as brilliant as *Seinfeld*. Not only did I learn how to write sitcoms from the masters, but those guys involved each writer in every aspect of the show. They included us in the process from start to finish: casting, editing, wardrobe, props, even down to attending the final sound mix. That doesn't happen on most shows, and how fortunate I was to be taught all those essential elements of TV production right out of the gate.

The show was the very definition of lightning in a bottle. Where can you even find actors like Jerry, Jason Alexander, Julia Louis-Dreyfus, and Michael Richards, let alone all on the same show? The synergy of those four together created a once-in-a-lifetime cast. And Jerry and Larry had an amazing chemistry of their own. I liken it to the partnership of Lennon and McCartney: Larry's more cynical and sullen perspective mixed with Jerry's sunny and pop sensibility. The combination was comedically lethal. I had so much fun every day that on the weekends, at a party or some other event with whomever I was with, I'd inevitably turn to them and say, "I have a much better time at work."

It's funny that my inexperience as a writer turned out to be the biggest advantage I had going when *Seinfeld* came a-knocking. Not just because Larry and Jerry were looking for writers free of the sitcom way of working, but also because it freed me to focus on pitching my ideas and figuring out why some worked and others didn't. And it was my experience as a woman that kept me on track in finding story ideas, which kept me employed for more than seventy-five episodes.

Keep your ideas concise, and you'll find it much easier to pitch them to the appropriate person. (If it helps, pretend you're pitching to Larry David and his arm's already in motion.) Keep alert for ideas rooted in your own life experiences or from those unsolicited suggestions that come your way (even if it means smiling politely at the 99.9 percent that are totally useless). Keep track of your ideas after you pitch them, so you can learn why some fly and some land with a thud. Also keep a little notebook with you all the time—I've been doing so since the first time I set foot onstage in 1977—because you never know when inspiration will strike.

And one last piece of advice: when you relocate, be careful to remove your prized memorabilia before the movers on the premises. Something I seemed to miss in the Mayflower Movers pamphlet.

## You Can't Have Any New Old Friends

*Seinfeld* set the gold standard for television comedy, and even if it's a career high not likely to be repeated, my time on that show nevertheless taught me lifelong lessons about how to write comedy. The experience also taught me how to be a boss. Larry and Jerry were the easiest showrunners (biz lingo for the executive producers in charge of it all) I've ever worked for. They were always fair, direct, and generous with everyone on the set. They never treated a crew member differently from one of the network suits. I've tried to emulate that attitude whenever I'm in charge of a show and staff. (I'll talk about the very best boss I ever had—my father—later in the book.)

This situation is especially notable because it all took place during the era of the stand-up comedian in network TV. I heard plenty of stories from writers on other comedian-centered shows (*Roseanne, Grace under Fire*) that would make your head spin. But Jerry Seinfeld never had the requisite hissy fits or ego trips that went with a lot of his contemporaries. For him, the show was all about the work (he had the same attitude, from day one, as a stand-up comic). He knew that with his name as the show's title, it was up to him to set the tone. To this day, he remains the most un-hung-up person I've ever known, and without a day of therapy.

Earlier I mentioned the most common question I get, "What's Jerry Seinfeld really like?" (see Chapter 9, "The Singer, Then the Ventriloquist, Then the Chick"). I'll take a moment to

Julia Louis-Dreyfus, in Jerry and Larry's office after a taping, kicking back.

address it here, since we've been talking about the show. Simply put, Jerry's a mensch. (That Yiddish word, "mensch," is so much better than merely saying "nice guy," isn't it?) A buddy who's always been there for me in countless ways. Here's a great example.

One day a few years back, when I was in Los Angeles, I got a distressing phone call from my mom on Long Island. My dad had taken a fall outside their house, hit his head, and had some dementia as a result. He was taken to a hospital in Mineola to recover. Needless to say, I was a wreck.

Jerry happened to call soon after the conversation with my mom, and I filled him in on the bad news. "Well the *good* news is," Jerry said, "I'm scheduled to go back to New York tomorrow.

Why don't you come with me on my private jet"—the dude has worked hard over the years—"and when we land, you can go out to Long Island and see your dad." I was ecstatic with his generous offer and, of course, grabbed it.

The next day we boarded Jerry's jet—and if you've never flown privately, I really encourage you to try to have friends who are so successful that they've earned this perk in life. Jerry had lox and bagels on board, fresh from Nate and Al's Deli in Beverly Hills, and the fun plane ride certainly took my mind off my ailing dad whom I was so anxious to see.

We landed a few hours later, and off to Winthrop Hospital in Mineola I went. When I arrived, my dad was doing so much better than I had hoped—he was way more lucid than I'd imagined, with just some bumps and bad scrapes. My pop was so happy to see me, and I shared the story with him and my mom of how Jerry had graciously lent me a ride. (The folks always ate the show biz stuff up with a spoon!) When I left the hospital that night with my mom, we were both very encouraged by my dad's progress.

The next morning, I arrived at the hospital in an upbeat mood. I ran into the nurse and asked how my father was doing.

"Oh, not too good this morning," she said. "We've definitely taken a step backward."

"Oh, you're kidding," I replied dejectedly. "But he was doing so well yesterday!"

"No, no, the dementia's back," the nurse said. "Your

father woke up this morning talking about how his daughter flew in on Jerry Seinfeld's private jet, eating lox and bagels at thirty thousand feet . . ."

So even though he was almost responsible for an extended hospital stay for my dad, they don't come better than Jerry. Friends are so important—they help keep you sane every day as you brave the mercurial working world. Where would any of us be without them? If you have a Seinfeld or two in your life—and I mean a mensch, with or without a private jet—hold on to them. The saying "you can't have any new old friends" is a sage one.

The ceremonial "draw a line through the episode title" after taping.

On set with Estelle Harris and Jerry Stiller, "the Costanzas."

# CHAPTER 16

## KEEP YOUR SOUR CREAM OFF THE COUNTER

After writing for *Seinfeld*, there was only one television show I wanted to work on in the worst way: *The Larry Sanders Show*. I was a huge fan, and no other comedy captured my imagination like that show did.

I was in a good position to get hired. I knew Garry Shandling from my stand-up days. The first time we met (by the elevator in 30 Rock as I left a *Letterman* appearance), he complimented me on a joke I did, and it made my day. (The joke was about how ridiculous it is at the airport when they ask you, "Did you do all your own packing?" My response being, "Of course. Like most people, I use Mohammed's Packing Service.") Plus, just coming off writing for *Seinfeld* certainly didn't hurt either.

So, my agent got me a meeting to interview for the coexecutive producer position. The show was specifically looking to hire a woman. Now, sometimes that intention is good—those in charge truly care about adding female voices to the mix. Other times, they're doing it only because they have to. But regardless of the circumstances, when that's the objective, I'm always ready to prove it's the right decision.

Anyway, I went in to this interview well-armed. If there's one thing I learned from *Seinfeld*, it's that ideas are the gold that set good writers apart. (I also learned that Red Vines are delicious candy and hard to resist when showcased in a big plastic tub.) If you hand the star of a show or the showrunner a unique idea, you've got a serious foot in the door.

The day of the meeting, I did my usual. I went to the gym to get the *shpilkes* out (as my tribe says). I was pleased that I was scheduled for late morning, having always felt that being scheduled before lunch makes for a better meeting. After lunch, I feel like the other party is either reliving their meal or second-guessing their order. I was ready, and I went in pumped and positive.

When I walked into the room, Garry was there, as was the showrunner John Riggi (multiple Emmy winner from *30 Rock*). I knew and liked John, a fellow stand-up from back in the day. Our banter up front was light and fun, and we were off to a good start. I went on to talk about my passion and enthusiasm for the show. I was familiar with the previous season's episodes and touched on a few specific ones that I particularly loved. The meeting was going great.

So I decided to pull out the big guns (not those guns, you pervert): I told Garry and Riggi that I had some ideas for the upcoming season, and I asked if I could share a few. They were happy to hear them. Then the best thing that can happen during an impromptu pitch session happened—Garry and Riggi started to run with a few of my ideas, and soon we all started spit-balling together.

As we wrapped things up, Gary and Riggi told me they had a few more meetings to take with other writers but would know something definitive by the end of week.

I left that meeting flying. I phoned my agent as I pulled out of the building; this one was easy to call a ten. Even better: later that day, my agent followed up with the Sanders camp, and their feedback was amazing. (There's nothing worse than being the only one who thought a meeting was a ten. Although having the back of your dress tucked into your pantyhose after leaving the ladies' room is a very close second.) I was confident that by the end of the week, I'd be the new hire at *The Larry Sanders Show*.

The week ended with no news. Not unusual. Another week went by, still no news. My agent was told they were "still thinking about it." Then two weeks turned into four weeks, with the assurance of "it's looking good." But I wondered if that was truly the case. In business, I've come to learn that the longer you have to wait for a decision, the worse it is. Sour cream left out on the counter for a few hours ain't going back to the fridge. Or so said my Grandma Becky.

Larry David even offered to call Garry to put in a good word for me, and I gratefully took him up on it. Finally, a week before the start of the new TV season, I heard they'd hired another woman for the coexec position. I was devastated. After all those weeks of stringing me along and keeping my hopes up, this was such a stone-cold bummer.

A few months later, Paul Reiser was hired to host the Emmys and asked me to write for him. Lo and behold, the night of the awards, who did I run into but Garry Shandling. We talked for a while, and then the subject turned to his show. I shared how disappointed I was that I didn't get the gig, and how I believed I could have really made a difference there. Garry was very gracious about it. Then, completely out of the blue, he asked, "If something were to come up where a position became available, would you still be open to it?" "Absolutely!" I gushed, even though I seriously doubted that would ever come to pass. I thought he was just being nice.

A month later, my agent got a call. The woman writer they had hired wasn't working out, and they asked me to come onboard. I was thrilled. Even better, my time on Garry's show turned out to be phenomenal, even resulting in an Emmy nomination. Garry is not only an amazing actor but a brilliant writer/producer, with an innate sense of scene structure and dialogue that is uncanny. I learned so much from him. *The Larry Sanders Show* was also my first experience with the classic sitcom "writers' room." I got to experience the beauty of it, the remarkable synergy of all that comic energy in one room. One idea leads to another, and the volley never stops until a joke or a scene achieves its best evolution.

It's really hard not to take things personally in show business. When you're rejected, it's you someone doesn't want, there's no way around it. It plays to your insecurities, and insecurity in this business is as common as the name Jayden in a Santa Monica preschool.

But I've thought a lot about this Garry Shandling story over the years. I could have held a grudge about being rejected. I could have developed an attitude about them stringing me along all those weeks and then ultimately not giving me the job. But how would that have served me? What I wound up doing when I saw Garry— being friendly and sharing, in an honest but light-handed way, that I was bummed not to get hired—turned out to be exactly the right thing to do.

Disappointments are fast and furious in show business. And, unfortunately, I'd say the bad experiences often outweigh the good ones. I imagine the same is true in most vocations. Most of us hear "no" far more often than "yes," and it never feels good to be turned down. When the inevitable rejections happen, it's healthy to get out your anger and bitch and moan and vent. But do it to your friends and family—or the guy at Starbucks you're now unfairly ahead of in line because he politely held the door for you—or to whomever is your designated crap receptor. Then move on.

In other words, don't hold a grudge. Don't turn bitter when an opportunity doesn't pan out. Sour cream belongs in the fridge, not out in the open where everyone can see it spoil. In the business world, bringing your sour grapes wherever you go is only slightly more attractive than pulling out a piece of floss and whaling on your gums during lunch.

Photo ©1997 WB NETWORK.
All rights reserved. Permission is
hereby granted to reproduce this
photograph for publicity, promotion
or advertising connected with the
program depicted herein and for no
other purpose. Not for sale.

ALRIGHT
ALREADY

(Clockwise L-R) Amy Yasbeck as
Renee; Stacy Galina as Jessica
Lerner; Jerry Adler as Alvin Lerner;
Maury Sterling as Vaughn Lerner;
Mitzi McCall as Miriam Lerner; Carol
Leifer as Carol Lerner

# CHAPTER 17

## AGAIN WITH THE FAILURE?

If you're not failing, you're not doing something right.

So there I was. This was the night I'd been waiting for. The pinnacle of my career. I was starring in my own pilot for a sitcom that I had written and created.

My nerves before the evening's taping were off the chart. I was shooting on the same lot as *Seinfeld*, so Jerry came by for moral support. He could see how nervous I was and he said, "You know, there's not just one thing, Carol."

I shrugged, and he correctly figured out that I had no idea what he meant. He continued:

"Take the pressure off yourself. It feels like the most important night of your life, but it's really just another night in the bigger picture of everything you do. Now, go have fun out there." (That last piece of advice is the one he's always given me, ever since my first *Letterman* shot.)

At first, I thought Jerry was being a bit of a buzzkill. "Of course, it's the most important night of my life! I'm shooting a pilot for my OWN SHOW."

But seventeen years later, I see the wisdom of Jerry's advice. Yes, there are highly pressurized, important moments in anyone's career. But the key at those times is to see the long game. Because that, and not a single moment, is what ultimately defines the course of your career.

In the end, it did turn out to be a great night. The pilot we shot went on to be picked up. But my sitcom *Alright Already* ran on the WB network for only one season. We had amazing reviews that I'm still so proud of, from many top critics, but it was a "ratings-challenged" show (as most everything was on that fledgling network).

I still remember getting a big laugh at the "upfronts" that year in New York City. (An upfront is a meeting where new shows are introduced by the network to advertisers and the press.) When they announced my show and I stood up to say a few words, I said, "A lot of people put down the WB. But I'm here to tell you, I'm taking this show all the way to number a hundred and eighteen!"

So, do I look back on the experience as a failure because *Alright Already* got canceled? Not for a moment. (Okay, maybe for a moment.) I met some great writers and crew with whom I continue to work to this day. I learned invaluable lessons about being a boss and the importance of having a strong support team in place. And I had a ton of laughs in the process. "Not just one thing" indeed.

Writing this book has been a real time trip for me because

so many of the things I'm anxious to give advice about are things I wish I had known when I was starting out. I'd love to be able to go back in time and tell my younger self all I that I know now. (And tell her to invest in Apple.) But the biggest piece of advice I'd want to impart to the young Leifer—and to whatever-age-you-are you—is about failure. Because when I was young, I was terrified of failure. And that fear can stop you dead in your tracks, especially when you're attempting something creative. Yet, the only way to become successful at anything is to fail. And here's the kicker—to fail over and over and over. (Okay, maybe just two "overs.")

Amy Poehler said this in an *Entertainment Weekly* article in 2013: "Be okay with writing really bad stuff for a long time—just keep doing it. The act of doing it, the muscle memory of it, is more important than how it is. That's why improv was so instrumental for me, because you would do shows every night, and they would suck every night, and one night they'd be okay, and it would sustain you for another year." Or how 'bout this amazing quote from director Mike Nichols? When Elaine May asked him in a January 2013 *Vanity Fair* interview "What have you learned?" Mike responded, "I've learned that many of the worst things lead to the best things, that no great thing is achieved without a couple of bad, bad things on the way to them, and that the bad things that happen to you bring, in some cases, the good things."

Although I'll admit that it's still a personal challenge, it's important to be open to constructive criticism, too—from others, and even from yourself. Learning from that kind of input can drastically lessen the amount of failure you'll encounter moving forward.

For example, as a writer I've come to learn my strengths but also my weaknesses. I think I'm best with dialogue and jokes, but story structure still remains a bear. So I make sure that when I'm staffing a show, I have a solid structure writer in the room to compensate for my deficiencies. I think my writing started to get much better when I acknowledged that this was a place I could really use the backup.

The other thing about failure is that, with some tweaking, many times you can turn the situation into a win.

I was dying to be on NBC's *Celebrity Apprentice*. I was a true fan and watched the show religiously. I loved the tasks that were thrown at the celebrities and the ensuing strategy and alliances that were formed. And being so passionate about animal rescue, the idea of raising an insane amount of money for my charity, the North Shore Animal League, was extremely compelling. So when I finally got cast on the show, I was convinced I was going to seriously kick some ass. I mean, please! I was playing with the likes of rocket scientist Bret Michaels. My only fear going in was being the first one fired—no one wants to be that loser.

Well, cut to me being the first one fired. (Does it really matter why? *Upstairs/Downstairs* the show is not.) As I heard my name falling out of Donald Trump's mouth, my head was reeling.

"Holy crap! Is this really happening?!" My worst nightmare, confirmed. But in that split second, I made a decision. Over my dead body was I leaving without something for my nonprofit. So I went for it:

"Mr. Trump?" I asked. "When we started this competition, you said you were a fan of my charity."

"I did," said Trump. "I admire the work of the North Shore Animal League very much."

"So, would you consider making a donation to them?" (Remember "You don't ask, you don't get," from Chapter 2?)

"Absolutely," said Trump. "I'll give you ten thousand dollars for them."

Bam! And with that, I left that show a winner. (And Donald Trump did make good on his promise; he sent a check to North Shore from his personal account. Believe me, I checked.)

P.S. I think using the word "consider" helped me enormously in my ask for a donation.

P.P.S. Bret Michaels went on to win, even though I think he stole my eyeliner.

P.P.P.S. Little fun fact: After you get fired from *Celebrity Apprentice*, the producers offer you therapy if you want it. "No thanks, guys! I think I'll be able to handle being fake fired from a fake job."

So, go ahead. Fall on your face. Wipeout. Crash. A lot. As any successful person will tell you, it's par for the course.

On the set of *Celebrity Apprentice*.

With Lori and my mom on the set of *Alright, Already.*

# CHAPTER 18

## RESPECT YOUR YODAS

There are legends in every business. And in my business of show, I've been lucky enough to interface with some special ones.

So I was very excited one day when my bud Paul Reiser suggested a double-date trip to Vegas with him and his wife to go see Bill Cosby. Paul had seen his stand-up concert a year earlier and was way impressed. Especially with the fact that Cosby did close to two hours of material with no break or opening act. Paul also knew Bill personally, so he made all the arrangements for the tickets, which was a lovely perk. I got even more psyched for the trip when Paul told me that he had secured backstage passes as well.

Cut to the Bellagio hotel. We enjoyed a nice dinner before the show—Paul and his wife, Paula, myself and my partner, Lori. (Well, as nice a dinner as you can have twenty feet away from a bank of slot machines. My brain continuously repeated the *Wheel of Fortune* theme for the next hour, easy.) After dinner, we headed to the showroom at the Aladdin and took our seats. (Dead center, three rows back. Love being a friend of a friend!) Then, around ten minutes before the eight p.m. curtain time, one of

Bill's people suddenly appeared at our seats and asked to bring us backstage. Oh, I guess we're getting to say a quick hello to Mr. Cosby sooner than I thought! He whisked us from our row, and we all headed to Cosby's dressing room.

We walked inside and Bill was immediately warm and friendly. He told me he was familiar with my work as a stand-up comic, and I tried to keep my cool even though inside I was freaking out. After a few minutes of idle chit-chat, most of it Paul and Cosby catching up, I looked at my watch to see that it was now a few minutes past eight. *I guess I had the showtime wrong*, I thought to myself.

Bill invited us to sit down, even offering us some drinks. As he sat, Bill turned to Paul and me and asked, "So what do you want to know?" I was slightly confused by the question, and sharing a surreptitious glance with Paul, I could tell he was feeling the same.

"About stand-up," Cosby clarified. "What do you want to know?"

After a beat of awkward silence, I launched right in.

"Well, I must say that when I watch you, Mr. Cosby—"

"Call me Bill . . ."

". . . when I watch you perform in your specials, I'm always amazed that you not only sit down onstage when you do your act, but that when you get up on your feet, you stay in one spot. I find that if I'm not moving and pacing the stage when I do my stand-up, I feel like I'll lose the audience."

Bill nodded and then went on to share his thoughts—how sitting onstage is a confidence thing that evolves with time. How the more secure you feel as a performer, the more secure you are in physically rooting yourself. He said that he felt it's a sign of strength in a performer when he or she can hold the audience with just his or her energy, as opposed to trying to rouse the energy of the crowd.

I hung on to every word, as did everyone else, sensing this rare opportunity at the feet of our personal Yoda, eager to share his wisdom. I remember Paul jumping in next (what else could he do, he was clearly on deck!) and Cosby having a very thoughtful answer . . . but for the life of me, I don't remember Paul's question. (I even checked with Paul while writing this chapter, and he doesn't remember either!)

All I knew was, when I next looked up at the clock on the dressing room wall, it was eight-thirty. Bill's guy subtly signaled that it was time to go, so naturally we all got up to give Bill his privacy. I was surprised to see that when we did that, Bill got up, too, and exited the dressing room right along with us. The next thing I knew we were all walking backstage, and as Bill said a nice goodbye, the curtains parted and he walked out onstage to thunderous applause. We were led back to our seats (our late entrance making the members of our row squirm uncomfortably) and then went on to enjoy Cosby's phenomenal show.

Meeting Bill Cosby was like meeting Yoda . . . a taller, funnier Yoda.

The truth is, the show *did* start at eight p.m., with our little backstage chat, which was responsible for the late onstage start. I guess I should have seen that coming—when you're confident enough to sit onstage with the audience hanging on to every word, you're probably confident enough to go onstage whenever the hell you want! To be honest, when we sat down I worried that the audience was going to be in a testy mood. But the minute Bill stepped out he was off and running, and no one gave a second thought to the late start. Maybe they should change that slogan to "What happens in Vegas, usually happens a half hour later than scheduled in Vegas."

Other bouts with greatness are achieved only after a true test of patience.

To my generation of comics, appearing on *The Tonight Show* with Johnny Carson was the pinnacle of success. It was a time when an appearance on that show could turn you into a star overnight: Freddie Prinze, Roseanne, Drew Carey—the list of comics who made their bones on that show is impressive.

Needless to say, I wanted to be on *The Tonight Show* more than anything. My first audition was back in 1981, at the Comic Strip. The show's talent producer, a guy named Jim McCauley, came in to check out the stand-ups who were part of the club's showcase. I had a great set that night and was optimistic that I might just have scored myself a booking. But word came back to the club about those Jim was interested in (I didn't have an agent at the time), and my name wasn't one of them.

Who knew that my first audition for *The Tonight Show* would one day lead to twenty-two more auditions over the course of eleven years—all universally ending with "no, thanks." I just couldn't figure it out. I always had a good show when Jim came in, sometimes really killing it. I made sure to change up my material each time, so he would see new stuff. It got to the point where I would change some minute variable each time he came back, like wearing a dress or putting on a pair of heels, just to see if that would seal the deal. Still, all I ever got afterward was rejection.

It sure got frustrating, and it tested me, but nothing was

ever going to stop me from giving it another shot. I always went into it thinking, *Maybe this time, who knows?* Other comics told me they thought McCauley wasn't putting me on because I was too closely identified as a *Letterman* regular, but Paula Poundstone segued to and from both shows easily. After a while, I simply got tired of asking myself "why?"—it was wasted energy.

But looking back, I realized that I unknowingly followed the advice I'm trying to give so often in this book: I didn't let the rejection defeat me. Was it discouraging? Absolutely. But this was business, so I just kept my head down and kept working.

Soon Jay Leno started guest hosting a lot for Johnny, and he asked me to be in a sketch on the New Year's show when he was filling in, a takeoff of the old dating show *Love Connection*. The producers, including Jim McCauley, were very happy with what I did. And lo and behold, a month later McCauley finally invited me to appear on the show as a stand-up. What changed, eleven years later? I think I just outlasted them. I had achieved a certain measure of success on my own without *The Tonight Show*, and I believe I finally got rewarded for that.

Doing the show was a blast. After my set (which went extremely well), Johnny called me over to "The Couch," which was a big deal back then. I was lucky enough to be on the panel alongside the great Bob Newhart. Our repartee was smooth and fun. During the commercials, a couple things occurred that still stand out in my mind. First, while watching at home,

I always noticed Johnny tap his pencil along to the beat when Doc Severinsen and the Tonight Show Band played during the commercial breaks—Johnny was, after all, a drummer. Well, in person, seated two inches away, I noticed that Johnny's drumming was crazy loud and at a manic pace. Second, Johnny complimented me on one of my jokes, which I'll never forget. I used to do this one: "I don't have any kids. Well, at least none that I know about . . ." During the break, Johnny turned to me and said, "Nice switch on that joke. Good one!"

So, respect the greats, in whatever business you choose. Know who they are and what you would discuss with them if you could. Sometimes an opportunity to interact with a Yoda of your industry falls in your lap, and you don't want to miss a chance to glean some wisdom. Other times, you'll have to work really hard to get that opportunity, but the motivation to share a few moments with a legend can bring out your best work. I'll add that after almost forty years in my profession, I now see this situation from the perspective of an old-timer. And I realize that it's nice to be acknowledged for whatever contribution you make to your field.

Always have a question ready, though. That way when a legend asks, "So, what do you want to know?" you'll be prepared.

**PART THREE**

HOW TO KEEP YOUR FOOTING

WHEN YOU FINALLY GET A LEG UP

TO THE TOP OF THE HEAP

"Carol, you never know . . ."

—Anna Leifer, PhD

# CHAPTER 19

## THANK YOU, STAND-UP COMEDY!
## I'LL BE HERE EVERY WEEK

Not long ago, I went down to the Laugh Factory (where there's one assembly line working on set-ups, the other on punch lines), a comedy club on the Sunset Strip, as I occasionally do to try out material. The owner, Jamie Masada, is an old friend who is always great about the "drop in" that comics like to do. Jamie slated me for ten minutes, following a guy I go way back with named Tom Dreesen.

The emcee was on as I walked in, warming up the crowd. And I could see this group was not an easy one to wrangle— no surprise since it was a Friday, the worst comedy night of the week. The Friday crowd is filled with people who've been working hard (or just working) for the past five days, and all they want to do is get trashed and do it quickly. This was a particularly young crowd, too, making the room feel like a high school cafeteria that served drinks.

The emcee was struggling; he couldn't get the audience to focus or be quiet. Instead of doing his job—his only job, making sure the crowd's in the zone before bringing up the first act—he bailed. He brought Tom right up onstage, as if to say, "You get 'em quiet, dude, 'cause I sure can't!"

Tom struggled the first few minutes—how could he not when the emcee left the audience in that state? But staying the course like a pro, and pounding the crowd with a steady round of good solid jokes, gray-haired Tom eventually won them over. And as I watched these young faces (some no doubt the age of Tom's grandkids) surrender to the laughs, I thought to myself: that's the beauty of the vocation I chose. In comedy, it doesn't really matter how old you are, or any number of other variables. What matters is if you're funny. Period. You tell your jokes, and the audience laughs or they don't. Pretty simple.

Oh, my schadenfreude when I see these poor schnooks who have to retire from sports or modeling when they hit old age at thirty. It's not even an option for them; it's an inevitability. But not my tribe. If you're still getting a response from the audience, you're still in the game. Yep, I chose my profession well.

Not a day goes by that I'm not thankful I chose to start out as a stand-up comic. It was the smartest decision I ever could have made at the ripe old age of twenty-one. And even though my career has taken me in many diverse directions since then—as a writer, as a corporate speaker, and as a spokesperson—I could not have asked for a better foundation. Being a comedian has given me a priceless skill set for life and for the work world in general.

Gratitude feels good. No doubt your own profession has graced you with a useful tool kit to be grateful for (literally, if you happen to be a carpenter). If you've been at it a while, I especially urge you to take an inventory as a way of reconnecting with what you love about what you do. Sometimes we get so caught up in the tangible rewards that come with a career—how much money we make, how nice our office is, how many free lunches we can wheedle—that we overlook the intangible ones. So make your list.

I'll start with mine:

## 1. It takes a lot to spook me.

Ask your average person what his or her greatest fear is, and most will say "talking in front of large groups of strangers." Ask your average comedian what their greatest fear is and most will say "not talking in front of large groups of strangers."

Comedians are warriors. You have to be to become successful. As a result, we're a pretty bulletproof assortment. It's hard to be fazed once you've faced a roomful of drunks daring you to be funny.

That's why, when people ask if I'm afraid when I go into a network president's office to pitch a new show, they're surprised to hear that I truly look forward to it. Please! I'm pitching to a captive audience of maybe four people (depending on how many kiss-asses the big cheese likes to have around) who are sober (or at the very least not ordering drinks while I'm talking) and who are paid to be somewhat interested in what I'm saying. Believe me, as a "friend" once told me, when you've eaten it as a stand-up comic in front of twenty thousand people, following seven hours of acts at a comedy festival in San Francisco, entertaining four suits is a piece of cake. So feel free to contact me if you have an iffy return situation you've been avoiding at a department store. I'm confident I'll get your money back, with a gift card to boot. Low-level confrontations make my day.

Fortunately, that quality also extends to staying calm in the face of danger. My partner, Lori, has often commented over the years about how cool I am in the pressured situations we've shared together. That only comes from vigorously protecting my own ass onstage all these years. (See my "Beach Boys-bombing-in-Lake Tahoe" incident, Chapter 7, and you'll know why staying calm when my car broke down in the left lane of the 5 Freeway, with failing hazard lights, during rush hour, was no biggie.)

## 2. I can read you like a book as easily as you're reading mine.

Working as a stand-up gives you a keen sense of people's attention and whether you've captured it (or not). Which is a crucial skill to master in any business—and doesn't hurt in your personal life, either. When you're onstage, you're constantly monitoring where the audience is, minute by minute. Sometimes you feel their energy flagging, and you need to counter that lapse by pumping up your own. Other times you sense them feeling neglected, so you take a few minutes to stop and talk to the audience to reengage them. And if you misread or lose them for a second, you can always count on a gentle reminder from someone out there (typically in the form of "You suck!").

One thing is for sure—no matter how badly you're bombing, you can never let the audience see its effect on you. You forge on as if everything is great. As Richard Belzer once advised me when I was starting out: "You're like the pilot of a plane up there. Once they see you panic, they're next." And that's also an invaluable business lesson for anyone.

It's funny, people's perceptions of what it's like to do stand-up comedy. I was opening for Jerry Seinfeld recently at the Civic Theatre in San Diego, and my partner Lori's cousin Jay came to the show with some friends. They had to leave early, but he sent me an e-mail later that night thanking me for the tickets and saying, "I don't know if you could hear the crowd or not, but they loved you!" I had to laugh. Oh, I heard them all right! If I'm not doing well up there, I'm the first to know! And while we're on the subject of people's misperceptions about stand-up comedy: no, we don't practice in front of a mirror.

## 3. The "business" will never define me.

Writing for television can be a real bear. There are so many ups and downs—you're hot one minute, and the next you're so ice cold you feel lucky if family members return your call. But the beauty of being a stand-up is that, when I have to endure these tough periods of rejection that rear their ugly head from time to time, my safety net is there to save me. I go down to the comedy club and I do a set. I have to after a day of being passed over for a writing gig, or of someone reading one of my scripts and telling my agent they don't think it's funny. It snaps me right back. Nobody can tell me they don't think I'm funny when a room full of strangers just told me otherwise. Whatever business endeavor you explore, I encourage you to find the thing that refreshes you and shores up your confidence, like doing stand-up does for me.

## 4. Building my career took a work ethic that started on the ground floor.

It may be surprising to hear, but every successful comedian I know has an extremely strong work ethic. That's because most comics write their own material. You learn early on that there's not much of a show until you sit your ass down and write yourself some jokes. So many people never get anywhere in business because their style is just to sit back and wait for others to start things up. As a comic, I learned right away the value of being an independent contractor.

When I first moved out to L.A. in 1982, Budd Friedman (the owner of the Improv) and his wife, Alex, hosted a barbecue for all the new comics who had recently moved out. Phil Foster, comedian, writer, and actor (Frank De Fazio of *Laverne & Shirley* fame), was a guest of the Friedmans and was BS'ing with a bunch of us. A buddy of mine was complaining about something or other, and I remember Phil shrugging and saying, "No one asked you to be in this business." I remember thinking at the time what a gruff response that was from this grizzled old-timer. (Hey, we're just eating some burgers and hot dogs over here!) But today I think the guy hit the nail on the head, and I might just say the same thing. Because it's not only good show business advice, it's good advice for whatever line of work you attempt. You put yourself in this business, and it's up to you to make it work.

So all this is to say, the next time you're at a comedy club on a Friday night, can you keep it down? I'm working up here!

# CHAPTER 20

## WALTER WHITE'S WORK ETHIC

When I cocreated Ellen DeGeneres's sitcom, *The Ellen Show*, we ran into a bit of a problem casting the role of Ellen's mom. We reached out to lots of A-list actresses and, as often happens, most of their agents came back to us with "offer only." Meaning, the talent is not open to auditioning. And that's especially frustrating because, as respected and famous as some actors are, the creator and writer of the show would still love to see them doing the part before offering them the role.

Well, after a couple weeks of trying, we weren't getting far because all these high-end actresses wouldn't even come in and read. That is, until Cloris Leachman. Yes, the Oscar winner, and one of my comedy idols, the woman who played Phyllis on *The Mary Tyler Moore Show*. Cloris came in and she not only auditioned, she hit it out of the park. (Plus, she's a pleasure and a delight in person.) And once Cloris came in and did that, she ruined it for everyone else. Because once someone of that stature has the balls (and sense) to come in person and do what actors do, all those "offer only's" didn't stand a chance. So never be shy; always be ready to dazzle people with your awesome talent, even if you think it's somewhat beneath you. Your ability and drive are what got you where you are in the first place. Never lose sight of that.

If I impart anything to you over the course of these chapters, I hope it's that finding what you love will make your life's work a joy. And my wish is that you find a career as satisfying as the one I have. But the big and surprising secret is: it never gets easy. The one misconception people have about my career is that every day I'm coasting. As if you achieve a certain measure of success, and then you simply glide along. Nothing could be further from the truth. It's not that way in my profession, and it's probably not in yours, either.

There's a reason for my career longevity, with no slowdown in sight. The reason is this: every day, I wake up and I'm at it. I'm relentless. And although having to push so hard may suck a good portion of the time—and I do get pissed at still having to prove myself after all this time—guess what? It comes with the territory. In any business, male or female, Cloris Leachman or not Cloris Leachman.

For example, I've written for the Academy Awards seven times, and I hope to do so many more times in the future. But do you think that every time the Academy people announce a new host, they just call me up and book me to write the show? Far from it. Each year I have to work tirelessly to get the gig

With Ellen DeGeneres on location for filming the pilot of *The Ellen Show*.

again. And if I decided to do anything less, then that many more writers would have a better shot at the job.

No industry supports a passive person. If you sit around and wait for the phone to ring, you might as well leave it on mute. And I've seen this situation grow much more intense over the years. It is so competitive and brutal and cutthroat out there that if I don't start the equation with one hundred percent of what I know I can bring to the table, I'll already be at a disadvantage. So many things along the way are poised to knock you down that bringing anything less than your best would be self-destructive.

No one hands you a career, ever. Even in my field, nobody gets "discovered" anymore. That ancient "Lana Turner sitting at Schwab's drugstore" mythology doesn't exist today. (Okay, maybe today's Lana Turner gets discovered by making a sex tape, and then gets "pretend mad" when it's released.) This theory is confirmed when someone like an Adam Lambert kills on *American Idol*, because he was a nuts-and-bolts working singer all those years before the competition. That prepared him for turning it up on the world stage. And Justin Bieber became a sensation only after he laid all the groundwork himself, working tirelessly making videos and doing live appearances anywhere and everywhere.

I'm often asked to speak at comedy classes or workshops. And the thing I'm most amazed at (besides the cost) is when the students tell me at the book signings afterward that it's their fifth or sixth time attending. Don't get me wrong, some of these classes are a good introduction to the craft—a place to feel comfortable and to work out the kinks. But there does come a time, with any venture, when the baby bird's got to leave the nest. Want to find out if you're funny? Go on stage and tell some jokes. Believe me, the audience will let you know. *Just do it.* (Kudos to Nike for an ad slogan that sums up one of the most existential and powerful keys to life.)

The great comedian Steven Wright gave me a piece of advice a year into my career that I'll never forget. He told me, "You've got to go up onstage every night for three years. *Three years*, with no judgment afterwards. And that's how you *start* to learn how to become a comedian." I was so consoled by Steven's words, because I regularly tore myself up after shows when I bombed—and I had plenty of those. The judgment so bad on myself that I was tempted many times just to quit.

So, whatever your profession, whatever resources you use to improve your skills—workshops, seminars, classes—don't try to be perfect before you use those skills in the real world. Just put on blinders and stick to the work. It's sound advice for any career journey. When you focus on that, you learn the invaluable lesson, to restate something I said a few chapters back: *Control what you can, and screw what you can't.* This is one of the most important mantras I want to share with you.

I first met Bryan Cranston, star of *Breaking Bad*, when he was a recurring guest star on *Seinfeld*. (Remember in the famous *Yada, Yada* episode when he played the dentist Tim Whatley who converts to Judaism, and Jerry thinks he did it just for the jokes?) Anyway, at the time Bryan wasn't the big star he is now, just a steadily employed bring-home-the-bacon-type actor. One day while making small talk with him on the set, I marveled about how a working actor like himself kept it together. Because I had a brief window, before my writing career took off, when my agent sent me out on some auditions. And I was miserable. Horrible at it on all fronts. And the worst part was, I would get completely obsessed after the audition, hounding my agent about feedback and checking in every five minutes to find out whether I got the part.

I remember Bryan telling me plain and simple, "Carol, I prepare like you wouldn't believe. Then I go in for the audition and I focus on giving them my best read. But once I leave that room of casting directors and producers, it's a distant memory as I leave the lot." Bryan told me that when his agent would call with a booking, many times he'd have to remind his client which part he had landed. Knowing that, and witnessing the amazing career Bryan has had since the *Seinfeld* days, why would you even wonder at it? He focused on what was important—the work.

Swim or die. Good advice for sharks, and for anyone who has to be in the water with them.

Bryan Cranston presents me with my Emmy nomination certificate
at the 2012 awards ceremony.

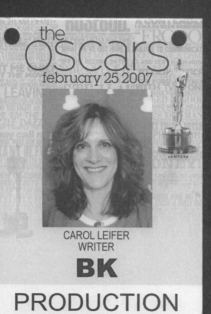

the **OSCARS**
february 25 2007

CAROL LEIFER
WRITER

**BK**

PRODUCTION

# CHAPTER 21

## THERE'S NO USE KVETCHING
## OVER YESTERDAY'S PICKLES

I get a call from my publicist one day. She tells me that a high-level entertainment magazine is doing a "Where Are They Now?" piece, and they want to profile me. My first thought: this request must not have made my publicist feel like a million bucks.

"Now why would I possibly want to be a part of a piece like that?" I ask her.

"Because any publicity is good publicity," she responds.

"Well," I say, "I'm not sure that I agree, when the name of the article could be 'You're So Out of the Business, We Can't Even *Find* You.'"

So I passed. About a week later, my publicist calls again.

"I spoke to them, and they assured me that it's not a has-been piece." (Like a contractor assuring that he'll come in at estimate.) "They asked if calling the piece 'Catching Up with . . .' would change your mind."

"Catching Up with . . . "? Okay, great. So now they've found me, but I'm just coming out of a coma.

Did I mention all this happened just eight years ago?

Never let them see you sweat? Nope. My motto is, Never let them see you buried.

I've had an amazing run in show business. Almost forty years in a business where ten would earn anyone bragging rights. A business in which women are still a minority, by far, and are routinely paid less than men. And in that time, there have been at least six or seven times (not including this week) when I just felt like it was *over*. I mean, dead in the water over.

But I've learned that in those times of extreme adversity, when the business is not only showing me the door but has dropped me by the curb to be whisked away to complete oblivion, it's my job to turn the situation around. I am way past my expiration date; most careers in my profession have the longevity of a prize won at a seaside arcade. Yet I still survive. Because in my heart, I know there's still so much more for me to contribute and accomplish.

*Rejection is an everyday part of business.* Recite that daily when you get up every morning, and you'll be one step ahead of the game. I'll admit, this is still a personal challenge for me. It's tough to be a sensitive person in an insensitive business. But I forge on, and so can you.

In some ways, rejection is easier to take early in your career, when you're green and you know you have a lot to learn. But whatever your occupation, never assume that once you pay your dues and reach a certain level of success, every door will be open to you. As I write this, I was just interviewed for a staff job on a sitcom, and afterward the producers asked my agent for "references." Now, a resume? Sure, completely reasonable. But "references"? Am I applying for work at Applebee's?

I'm turned down for jobs all the time. Let's take a look at an e-mail that one of my agents got from a bigwig at a very successful, Emmy Award–winning sitcom that recently ended its run. (This is after weeks of positive conversations with other bigwigs at the show regarding my joining the writing staff.)

- - - - - - - - - - - - - - - - - - - - - - - - - - - - - - -

**From**: XXXXXXXXXX [mailto:XXXXXX@XXXXXX.com]
[Sent: Monday, April 25, 9:37 AM
**To**: Katie
**Subject**: RE: Per our conversation/

Katie,

I lw for you…

Someone    has    been    calling    XXXXXXXXXXXXXXX
trying to schedule a Carol Leifer mtg on XXXXXXXX …
unfortuantley, it's just not the right fit.

Would you please pass this along to whomever has been calling him or his assistant? They can call me to discuss at any time.

Thanks,
XXXXXX

– – – – – – – – – – – – – – – – – – – – – – – – – – – –

Let's examine with a fine-toothed comb, since this is my book we're in . . .

– – – – – – – – – – – – – – – – – – – – – – – – – – – –

From: XXXXXXXXXX [mailto:XXXXXX@XXXXXX.com]
[Sent: Monday, April 25, 9:37 AM
To: Katie
Subject: RE: Per our conversation/

Katie,

I lw for you... ["So you know it's real important because I'm already e-mailing you after calling you."]

Someone ["Someone"? Implies a person who shouldn't have done it, like a ne'er-do-well janitor or maintenance man] has been calling XXXXXXXXXXXXXX trying to schedule a

Carol Leifer mtg on XXXXXXXX ... unfortuantley, [Spelled wrong] it's just not the right fit. [As in, a bucket of KFC at a PETA luncheon.]

Would you please pass this along to whomever [Again, implies a reckless wild card. Maybe an escaped convict found safe haven at a talent agency?] has been calling him or his assistant? ["I'm so serious about this, I'm even concerned about an assistant whose name I will never know."] They can call me to discuss at any time. ["But there's not a chance in hell they will, after hearing about this e-mail from you."]

Thanks,
XXXXXX

- - - - - - - - - - - - - - - - - - - - - - - - - - - - -

Here's the good news: You'll hear the word "no" a lot. But it only takes one "yes" to get you started on something new. And that's what drives me.

Believe me, when the time comes to leave the business, I'll know it. (Or at least I hope my aide will tell me). Because there's a lot to be said for a well-timed exit. Especially for the legends, it can be a delicate decision.

And some don't exactly get it right. The great Bob Hope was the host of a few "Young Comedians" specials on NBC late in his career, and I jumped at the chance to appear in one. Especially when legends like Milton Berle and Phyllis Diller were also booked. So the producers asked me to come up with a line to use when Hope and Milton Berle "outro-ed" me after my set. I took a joke from my act, about how everything was going so great for me that "I was offered a three picture deal . . . two eight by tens and one wallet." But poor Bob Hope couldn't hear a thing, and he was not in the best overall shape at this point. He just turned to me and exclaimed, "Good for you!" Yes, it was a thrill beyond compare to meet him and Milton Berle (I still treasure a couple of cue cards I have of their banter from the broadcast), but that moment made me just plain sad.

But until it's my time to bow out, bat me around all you want, business. I'm still here. (Cue song of the same name, sung by Elaine Stritch at the Sondheim birthday concert in 2010.) I just hope I never become bitter (or at least, bitter-er). Because you've got to have a sense of humor about your career to survive, that I know for sure. There's nothing worse than a table full of yammering AARP show business sourpusses at a deli who do nothing but complain about all the people who passed them by, and why the waitress refuses to put out the bright green pickles instead of the lifeless limp ones surely from yesterday's batch.

(Trust me, I overheard that just yesterday at Jerry's Deli in Studio City, with my still very well functioning ears.)

To Carol,
my Best
Bob Hope

# CHAPTER 22

## THE FISH STINKS FROM THE HEAD DOWN

So much of success in business is dependent on the attitude you bring to it. And if you're the one running the show, your attitude will definitely influence the attitudes of everyone else. Fortunately for me, the people who bossed me around the most—my parents—were two of the best possible role models for being a good boss. They showed me, by example, how important it is to value your profession and your workplace when you're the head honcho. Hopefully, your own parents have left some great tire tracks to follow on your path from small fry to Big Cheese. But if by chance your folks ran a meth lab out of a van in Tulsa, Oklahoma, feel free to use my parents as models. Trust me, Anna and Seymour would be more than happy about it.

My dad was an optometrist for fifty years. It was the profession he pursued after he got out of the army in 1945, and he continued in it until the day he died. He chose his field wisely, my pop, because he found optometry to be endlessly fascinating. Anything dealing with the eye and how it worked was, to him, off the charts (pardon the pun). That's not to say there wasn't another vocation he dreamed of. He wanted to be a comedian, or a comedy writer. But to men of his generation, working in entertainment was no more than that—a dream. "Making a living" was the nuts and bolts of real life. And he was quite content to be the cutup for his captive audience of patients. (With limited heckling, also a plus in that dark exam room.)

When I was a kid, Dad took the Long Island Railroad to his office in Manhattan every weekday. Later, when I was ten, he turned our garage into an office so that he could also see patients when he got home. (So much for my siblings and me starting a garage band.) It was, needless to say, a long day—patients all day in the city, and then three or four more at night. Some on Saturdays, too. Yet I don't remember him ever complaining. Well, at least not about work. The guy that sliced the lox down at the deli, that was another story. Anyway, even though it often meant he barely had time to grab a lamb chop with us for dinner, as soon as the office doorbell rang, Dad was off to work.

I don't think my father ever missed a day of work in his life. But when I look back, it's really no surprise. He truly loved what he did. He loved to tell stories about the various clueless types he encountered, like when he'd ask a patient to read the eye chart and the person would respond "Out loud?" Or the patients who would read the eye chart "Capital E, capital F, capital P . . . " Hysterical.

I got the best glimpse of my dad's work style when he

offered me a summer job as a receptionist. (I guess listing my mother as a reference worked.) Not only did I observe him doing his job, but I also got to check out what he was like as a boss and a businessman. I was one of three receptionists who worked the front desk at his office, which was then in Kew Gardens, Queens: greeting patients, checking them in, and retrieving or creating a "record card." Yes, on paper. Back then, computers took up an entire room and existed only at NASA or in sci-fi movies.

Pop was a good boss. True, for the first few days it was hard to make the switch to calling him "Dr. Leifer" instead of "Daddy." And hard to lose the habit of screaming "ALL RIGHT!" at the top of my lungs anytime he asked me to do something. In any case, it was obvious to me what a good boss my dad was. Here are five reasons why:

## 1. He treated customers like family.

His side of the family, anyhow. The minute people walked into his office, my father was friendly and warm. If we were backed up with patients, he would always say to the crowded waiting room, "Sorry for the delay, folks! We'll get to you all soon." He had a very positive, "up" energy, and it was infectious. In some ways, my dad was more easygoing as a boss than as a parent. He raised his voice a lot more often at home than in the office. (But then again, it's unlikely that one of his patients drank the last Tab from the rec room fridge.)

## 2. He felt that the customer was always right, especially when their volume was turned up.

In any business that deals with the public, there will always be somebody who's unhappy. At my local Starbucks, for example, it's usually me when I get the barista who's seen me every morning for the past three years and still asks for my name to write on the paper cup. (It's "Beyoncé," by the way.)

In my dad's office, many of these complaints were aired out loud, right at the front desk. But Pop was always cool with these disgruntled types. If a patient wasn't satisfied, he immediately set out to correct the problem. And I don't mean he was a pushover; he just felt that the customer's experience was paramount. I saw firsthand how important it is to simply *listen* to what the customers have to say. Sometimes, that was all it took to turn a bad situation completely around.

## 3. He was the first one in, the last to leave, and he liked to use fish metaphors.

My dad was always there to open the shop in the morning, and at the end of the day he was the one to lock up. I didn't realize how important that is until I'd held many jobs myself. But my dad knew that everyone takes their cue from the boss, or as he liked to say, "the fish stinks from the head down." (Fortunately, he didn't write his own wedding vows.) Pop felt responsible for his employees, and he believed the success of his business ultimately rested on his shoulders and his own hard work. If you have one of those bosses who breezes into the office at 11, takes a three-hour lunch, then leaves early "to meet with a client," take note of the resentment you're feeling, and remember it when you find yourself behind the big desk yourself.

## 4. He was tough, but decent, like a cheap steak.

My dad didn't tolerate bad behavior from his employees. Anyone who was late, or guilty of some other infraction, was thoroughly chastised. But Dad always made it clear what the consequence would be if there was a next time. It's a fair concept—you mess up again, well, you were warned. (Having a child of my own now, I truly see the value or this approach. Unfortunately, firing your child isn't usually a viable option.) But there's more to this story than just enforcing the ground rules. Because employees genuinely enjoyed working for my father, I could see that they truly felt bad when they disappointed him. That only comes when you work for someone you like and respect. So it was just as important that . . .

## 5. He created an equal playing field for all, including his baby girl.

Even though I was "the boss's daughter," my father never played favorites. At lunch time, for example, he always went out to eat. But I stayed back at the office, as all the receptionists did.

Funny quirk of his—my dad was diligent about staying trim, so his lunch every day was just an apple, and then he would walk down to the Kew Gardens courthouse and watch random trials. See what people were forced to do for entertainment before the Internet? Pop could easily have grabbed me and taken me along for company, but he didn't, because that would have been unfair to the other gals with whom I worked. (No matter to me. I loved staying inside, in the air conditioning. *You* try surviving Queens humidity in the summer!)

My mom gets her PhD from Yeshiva University, 1973.

My mom had her own great work journey. When I was in primary school, she took up teaching. But her dream was to become a psychoanalyst. So when I was in junior high, my mother attended Yeshiva University (bad Christmas parties, by the way) to get her doctorate in psychology. She received her degree in 1973 and soon after set up her own private practice, also in our home. Needless to say, my house was never the raucous party place. We had to be quiet at one end of the house for my dad's patients, and quiet at the other for my mom's. It's probably why I became a cheerleader in high school—it was the only place where I could yell.

My mother also taught at Adelphi University in Hempstead, Long Island, and over the years many of her students have come over to me at comedy shows to tell me what a wonderful and inspiring teacher she was. She kept seeing patients well into her eighties (my mom just turned ninety-four). So look out, Betty White, I'm hot on your tail! (I said, LOOK OUT, BETTY WHITE . . . oh, never mind.)

As a follower of Freud, my mother believed, as the good doc Sigmund did, that mental health means the ability "to love and to work." My parents certainly had the love part down, in that they were married for sixty-two years until my dad passed. And they were both very committed to the integrity and importance of work. They were both very "TGIM" (Thank God It's Monday) type people, and that quality was certainly passed down to me. A life without work would surely be an empty one.

One more thing you should know about my mom: as a parent, her shrink hat was always on. Usually in a good way. When I was sixteen and learning to drive, my mother would come with me when I practiced. Once I accidentally hit a squirrel in the road, and naturally I was upset about it. My mom consoled my by saying, "Don't give yourself a hard time about it, Carol. The squirrel clearly displayed suicidal tendencies."

Dad making glasses in his home office.

Newlyweds!

# CHAPTER 23

IN CLOSING:

MY TOP TEN PERSONAL THOUGHTS ON SUCCESS

When writing this book, I found major tent poles of success that kept reappearing throughout each chapter. So I thought I'd single out my most personal and favorites for you, so you can always refer to them. Believe me, even after almost forty years in business, I still need a Letterman-style list like this to remind myself of the big basics!

## 1. Don't dwell on failure.

Stewing over disappointments is wasted time that gets you nowhere. As Amy Pascal, cochairman of Sony Pictures, has eloquently said: "They won, you lost—move on."

## 2. The simple fact is, business is sexist.

So is just about everything else. And why boo-hoo about it when that won't change anything? Real change will come only when women make other women a priority: hiring them, mentoring them, promoting them, etc. In my experience, a climate of competition still pervades relationships among women, so if you want change, put your energy into changing that. There's still no "Old Girl's Club," but there should be.

### 3. Tenacity is a must to get ahead in anything.

The trick is to find the right balance. "The squeaky wheel gets the grease," but the squeaky wheel can also make someone say "screw it," toss the wheel in the trash, and go get a new bike. Be dogged, but not a pain in the ass. It's a fine line.

### 4. If you ask for donations, you have to give donations.

I learned that tenet from all my fund-raising adventures, though the same holds true in business settings. Before you ask for things from colleagues, remind yourself what you've done for them. There's a reason for the Latin phrase "quid pro quo." Don't expect quid if you never dish out any quo.

### 5. Don't be afraid of no.

It's one of my personal mantras. If you're okay with rejection—and you have to be in business—then you'll never be afraid to go after what you want. (Trust me, this quality is one that took me many years to learn.) But don't confuse this point with the saying "Don't take no for an answer." I'm all for persistence and tenacity, but the time comes when you have to accept a pass and move on. (And honestly, you should feel lucky when you finally get a definitive answer about something, even if it's a negative one. Being accountable is not high on most people's priority lists.)

## 6. Diversify.

When I was offered a writing job on *Saturday Night Live*, I almost didn't take it because I wanted the performer job I had auditioned for. But my dad sat me down, and we had a good long talk about how important it is to always look for ways to broaden a career. Especially with an opportunity as good as the one being handed to me. Dad knew that putting all my eggs in the one basket of stand-up comedy or acting would be risky over the long haul. He promised me I wouldn't regret the decision, and almost thirty years later I see how right he was. So, keep an eye out for chances to learn the ropes and gain new skills, even in matters that aren't your primary area of interest (yet).

## 7. "When the world Is running down, you make the best of what's still around."

I wish I had said that, and not Sting, but I think of this quote often in hard times. Riding the tough stretches of a career requires all the positive thinking you can muster. Always appreciate what you do have, instead of dwelling on what you don't.

## 8. Give criticism only after giving a compliment.

When you need to share an unpleasant truth, starting off with a solid validation helps a person take in your disappointment. I'm on both sides of this one all the time. It's a good rule of thumb for your personal life as well. "A spoonful of sugar helps the medicine go down" was a concept much vaster than what was conveyed in *Mary Poppins*.

## 9. Work on your craft every day.

With creative endeavors, this is especially important. The Muse needs to punch in every day, just like the rest of us. Whatever business you're in, undoubtedly there are specific skills that are critical to your success. Don't let those skills get rusty, even it means finding ways to hone them outside the workplace.

## 10. Learn to walk away when you get frustrated.

Don't keep banging your head against a wall. Take a break, and when you come back to the problem, you'll see the solutions more clearly. My dad taught me that a long time ago about solving crossword puzzles, and it's a great business lesson as well.

I'll always be grateful for Dave's support in those early days!

# SCRAPBOOK

Have you noticed all the photographs in this book? Because I never throw anything away, I have way more pictures and memorabilia than could possibly fit within these pages. The downside of this habit is that I might end up featured on an episode of *Hoarders*. The upside is that I have plenty to share, and there's room here for a few more mementos I thought you might enjoy.

At the Roslyn Country Club, 1962.
Six hours later, I finally got into the water.

The day the pyramid collapsed. Me as a cheerleader, back row, far right.

Backstage in Vegas, with Richard Belzer, 1982.

*An Evening With*

# PETER ALLEN

*also appearing* Comedian CAROL LEIFER

*Friday November 14*

*At* The Governor Morris Inn

*2 Whippany Rd., Morristown, N.J.  2 Shows—8 p.m. & 11 p.m.*
*for Further Information Call  201-635-4741*

*Tickets For Both Shows Available At*
*The Following Locations:*

Music Staff Record Shop
27 Elm St
Westfield 233-1448

Washingtunes Headquarters
79 Washington St.
Morristown 267-1688

Scotti's Record Shop
67 Main St.
Madison 377-8981
351 Springfield Ave.
Summit 277-3893

My first "big time" gig: opening for the late great Peter Allen, 1980.

> **Ladies' Night Out Review**
> PRESENTS
> A Debbie VanHorn
> production of
>
> # HOT FANTASIES
> — FOR WOMEN ONLY —
> featuring
> MALE DANCERS
> &
> COMEDIENNE **CAROL LEIFER**
>
> MONDAY NIGHT          TUESDAY NIGHT
> 8:00 p.m. & 10:00 P.M.      8:00 P.M. & 10:00 P.M.
>
> AT
> **Baby O Disco**
> 406 Boulevard
> Seaside Heights, N.J.
> **(201) 830-3036**

My brief stint as an emcee at male strip clubs. Classy.

With Chris Rock at Catch a Rising Star, New York City, 1987.

One of the sweetest and funniest people ever, John Candy,
who hosted HBO's 8th Annual Young Comedians show in 1983.

With Rodney Dangerfield at the taping of his "Nothin' Goes Right" special in 1988.
Man, I love that robe!

With the one and only Phyllis Diller at Rainbow and Stars, New York City, 1989.
Every time I saw her, she would always shriek, "Isn't doing standup the best?"

With my manager Laurie Lennard, outside the Ed Sullivan Theater
for the taping of my Showtime stand-up special, 1990.

2-15-91

Dear Carol,

Here are the forms for the cable disconnect and the Coast to Coast papers.

I'll make one more trip later this month to pick up the mail and forward it to you.

I just want to tell you how much I admire your ability to cope with the necessity for moving to California. Judging from my one day with the movers, this has been a terrific strain on you, but that didn't faze you in the least. You just took it in stride and did what had to be done —— something for which I'll always be proud of you.

Lots of luck in your new location. To quote "New York, New York" "if you can make it there, you can make it anywhere."

All the best,
Mom + Dad

My dad, making sure that I knew I had his support . . . and that he disconnected the cable.

231

On the *Seinfeld* couch with Michael Richards and writer Peter Mehlman.

The night Johnny Carson passed away, Jerry put together this dinner in Los Angeles at Dan Tana's restaurant. Left to right: Bill Maher, Chris Rock, Garry Shandling, Jerry Seinfeld, me, Jimmy Brogan, Larry Miller (standing), Jay Leno.

**THE TONIGHT SHOW**

## CAROL LEIFER

JIM McCAWLEY
WEDNESDAY
FEBRUARY 5, 1992

<u>CAROL LEIFER</u>

STAND UP    5.30

OUTCUE      "Touch that thing and twirl...Thank you very much."

PANEL.

YOU DID A JOKE ABOUT BEING DIVORCED...HOW LONG WERE YOU MARRIED?

        Four years, but a joke about why it
        should have been 5.  She'll also talk
        about the concept of getting annulled.

YOU DON'T DO IMPRESSIONS IN YOUR ACT, DO YOU?

        She does one impression of a nose job, and
        will ask the camera for a close up.

WHERE ARE YOU FROM?

        East Williston, Long Island.  She has a
        funny reference to the town which shows
        how long she's been doing stand-up.

IS IT TOUGHER BEING ON THE ROAD FOR A WOMAN?

        She has road material, and a joke about London.

---

CAROL LEIFER                    QUESTIONS

PANEL:

YOU DID A JOKE ABOUT BEING DIVORCED...HOW LONG WERE YOU MARRIED?

YOU DON'T DO IMPRESSIONS IN YOUR ACT, DO YOU?

WHERE ARE YOU FROM?

IS IT TOUGHER BEING ON THE ROAD FOR A WOMAN?

**My dressing room door card, and Johnny's desk notes, for my first appearance on**
*The Tonight Show.* **And you thought talk shows were ad-libbed!**

Seinfeld, Jerry Lewis, and me backstage at *Damn Yankees* on Broadway in 1995.

With Paul Reubens, a.k.a. Pee Wee Herman. His voice is not that high in person.

With George Carlin in 1998. So glad I got to meet him before his untimely passing.

With Steve Levitan, cocreator of *Modern Family*, at the Writers Guild Awards in 2012. Winners for Comedy Series and Episodic Comedy!

With Sarah Jessica Parker and Matthew Broderick
in the green room at the 2010 Oscars.

With Alec Baldwin at the 2010 Oscars. He hosted with Steve Martin, and
we were nominated for an Emmy.

With Billy Crystal on the set of his Broadway show *700 Sundays* in 2005.
I've written for Billy three times for the Oscars.

At the taping of Seinfeld's HBO special "I'm Telling You for the Last Time."
Left to right: Garry Shandling, Robert Klein, Jerry Seinfeld, George Carlin, Alan King, me,
George Shapiro and Howard West (Jerry's managers), George Wallace, Ed McMahon.
I felt so lucky to be among such greatness.

I met President Clinton when Max Mutchnick (cocreator of *Will & Grace*) held a benefit at his home to raise funds for the Clinton presidential library.

# ACKNOWLEDGMENTS

Steve Fisher: Thank you for making this happen, and for finding the right home for my book.

Jason Rekulak: Thank you for being a terrific editor. You gotta love a guy who watches other people's turtles when their owners go away on vacation.

My pals: Bill Kelley, Dave Boone, Cathy Rath, David Schneiderman, Ricky Strauss and Steve Altiere. Thanks for the extra sets of eyes and ears.

The dogs: Julius, Shelby, Maccabee, Albert, and Cagney. Sorry you were cast off to the guest house so often while I was writing! Your barking is adorable, but very distracting.

And most of all, to Lori and Bruno: You are my heart and soul. What would work be like without both of you to come home to every night?